KARMA YOGA

SWAMI VIVEKANANDA

SANAGE
PUBLISHING HOUSE

Paperback: 978-939156035-5

Printed by: Manipal Technologies Limited, Manipal

Sanage Publishing House LLP
Mumbai, India

sanagepublishing@gmail.com

CONTENTS

I. Karma In Its Effect On Character

The word Karma is derived from the Sanskrit "Kri," to do; everything that is done is Karma. Technically, this word also means the effects of actions. In connection with metaphysics it sometimes means the effects of which our past actions were the causes. But in Karma Yoga we have simply to do with the word "Karma" as meaning work. The goal of all mankind is knowledge; that is the one ideal placed before us by the Eastern philosophy. Pleasure is not the goal of man, but knowledge. Pleasure and happiness come to an end. It is the mistake of mankind to suppose that pleasure is the goal; the cause of all the miseries we have in the world is that men foolishly think pleasure to be the ideal. After a time, man finds that it is not happiness, but knowledge, towards which he is going, and that both pleasure and pain are great teachers, that he learns as much from evil as from good. As pleasure and pain pass before his soul they leave upon it different pictures, and the result of these combined impressions is what is called man's "character." If you study the character of any man, what is it really but the tendencies, the sum total of the bent of his mind?

You will find that misery and happiness were equal factors in the formation of that character. Good and evil have an equal share in moulding character, and in some instances, misery is a greater teacher than happiness. In studying the great characters that the world has produced I dare say that, in the vast majority of cases, it was misery that taught more than happiness; it was poverty that taught more than wealth; it was blows that brought out the inner fire, more than praise.

Now this knowledge, again, is inherent in man; no knowledge comes from outside; it is all within. What we say a man "knows," should, in strictly psychological language, be a man "discovers;" what a man "learns" is really what a man "discovers," the word discover meaning "he takes the covering from his own soul," which is a mine of infinite knowledge. We say Newton discovered gravitation. Was it sitting anywhere in a corner waiting for him? It was in his own mind; the time came, and he found it out. All knowledge that the world has ever received comes from the mind; the infinite library of the universe is in your own mind. The external world is simply the suggestion, the occasion, which sets you to study your own mind, but the object of your study is always your own mind. The falling of an apple gave the suggestion to Newton, and he studied his own mind; he rearranged all the previous links of his mind and discovered a new link among them, which we call the law of gravitation. It was not the apple nor anything in the centre of the earth. All knowledge, secular or spiritual, is in the human mind. In many cases it is not discovered, but remains covered, and when the covering is being slowly taken off we say "we are learning," and the advance of knowledge is made by the advance of this process of uncovering. The man from whom this veil is being lifted is the more knowing man; the man upon whom it lies thick is ignorant, and the man from whom it has entirely gone is all-knowing, the omniscient. There have been omniscient men, and, I believe, will be yet, and that there will be myriads in the cycles to come. Like fire in a piece of flint, knowledge is existing in the mind; the suggestion is the friction that brings out that fire. So, with all our actions our tears and our smiles, our joys and our griefs, our weeping and our laughter, our curses and our blessings, our praises and our blames with every one of them we find, if we calmly study our own selves, that they have been brought out by so many blows. The result is what we are; all these blows taken together are called "Karma," work. Every mental and physical blow that is given upon the soul to strike out the fire, to discover its own power and knowledge, is Karma, Karma being used in its universal sense; so, we are doing Karma all the time. I am talking to you; that is Karma. You are listening; that is Karma. We breathe; that is Karma. We walk, Karma. We talk, Karma. Everything we do, physical or mental, is Karma, and is leaving its marks upon us.

There are certain works which are, as it were, the aggregate, the sum total, of a large number of small works. If we stand near the seashore and hear the waves dashing against the shingle, we think it is such a great noise, and yet we know that one wave is really composed of millions and millions of minute waves; each one of these is making a noise, and yet we do not catch the sound of them; it is only when they become the big aggregate that we catch it. So, every pulsation of the heart is making work; certain works we feel, and they become tangible to us; they are, at the same time, the aggregate of a number of small works. If you really want to judge the character of a man look not at his great works. Every fool becomes a hero at one time or another. Watch a man do his most common actions; those are the things which will tell you the real character of a great man. Great occasions rouse even the lowest of human beings to greatness, but he is a really great man whose character is great always, the same wherever he be.

This Karma in its effect on character is the most tremendous power that man has to deal with. Man is a centre, as it were, and he is attracting all the powers of the universe towards himself, and in this centre is fusing them all and ejecting them again in a big current. That centre is the real man, the almighty, the omniscient, and he draws the whole universe towards him; good or bad, misery or happiness, all running towards him, clinging round him, and out of them he fashions the tremendous power called character and throws it outwards. As he has the power of drawing in anything, so he has the power of throwing it out.

All the actions that we see in the world, all the movements in human society, all the works that we have around us, are simply the display of thought, the manifestation of the will of man. Machines or instruments, or cities, ships, men-of-war, everything is simply the manifestation of the will of man, and this will is made by character, and character is manufactured by Karma. As is Karma, so is the manifestation of the will. The tremendous, willed men that the world has produced have all been tremendous workers gigantic souls, with wide wills, powerful enough to overturn worlds; and they got that by persistent work, through ages and ages. Such a gigantic will as that of a Buddha or a Jesus cannot be got in one life, for we know who their fathers were. It is not known that their fathers ever spoke a word for the good of mankind. Millions and millions of carpenters like Joseph have gone; millions are still living. Millions and millions of petty kings like Buddha's father have been in the world. If it is only a case of hereditary transmission, how do you account for this little petty prince, who was not, perhaps, obeyed by his own servants, producing this son, whom half a world worships? How do you account for this gap between the carpenter and his son, whom millions of human being's regards as God? It cannot be accounted for by that theory. This gigantic will which Buddha threw over the world, which came out of Jesus, whence did it come? Whence came this accumulation of power. It must have been there through ages and ages, continually growing bigger and bigger, until it burst on society in a Buddha or a Jesus, and it rolls down even to the present day.

And all this is determined by Karma, work. No one can get anything except he earns it; this is an eternal law; we may think it is not so, but in the long run we shall be convinced of it. A man may struggle all his life in becoming rich; he may cheat thousands, but he finds at last that he did not deserve it, and his life becomes a trouble and a nuisance to him. We may go on accumulating for our physical enjoyment, but only what we earn is ours. A fool may buy all the books in the world, but they will be in his library, and he will only be able to read those he deserves, and this deserving is produced by Karma. Our Karma determines what we deserve and what we can assimilate. We are responsible for what we are, and whatever we want ourselves to be we have the power to make ourselves. If what we are now has been made by our own past actions, it certainly follows that whatever we want to be we can make ourselves by our present actions; so, we have to know how to act. You will say, "What is the use of learning how to work? Everyone works in this world." But there is such a thing as frittering away our energies. With regard to this Karma Yoga, in the Bhagavad Gita it is said that Karma Yoga is doing work, but with cleverness and as a science; knowing how to do work that will bring the greatest results. You must remember that all this work is simply to bring out the power of the mind, which is already there, to wake up the soul. The power is inside every man, and the knowledge is there; these different works are like blows to bring it out, to cause this giant to wake up.

A man works for various motives; there cannot be work without a motive. Some people want to get fame, and they work for fame. Others want to get money, and they work for money. Others want power, and they work for power. Others want to get to heaven, and they work to get to heaven. Others want to leave a name when they die, as they do in China, where no man gets a title until he is dead; that is a better way, after all. When a man does very good things they give a title of nobility to his father, who is dead, or to his grandfather. Some of the Mohammedan sects work all their lives to have a gigantic tomb when they die. I know sects among whom, as soon as a child is born, they begin to prepare for his tomb; that is the greatest work a man has to do, and the bigger and finer the tomb the better off the man is supposed to be. Others work as a penance; do all sorts of wicked things, then erect a temple, or give something to the priests to buy them off and give them a passport to heaven. They think that will clear them and that they will go scot-free. These are some of the various motives for work.

Work for work's sake. There are a few who are really the salt of the earth in every country and who work for work's sake, who do not care for name, or fame, or to get to heaven. There are others who do good to the poor and help mankind from still higher motives, because it is good, and they love good. Desires for name and fame seldom bring immediate results; as a rule, they come to us when we are old and are done with life. If a man works without any selfish motive in view what becomes of him? Does he not gain anything? Yes, he is the highest gainer. Unselfishness pays more, only people have not the patience to practise it. It is more paying in physical value also. Love, and truth, and unselfishness are not only moral figures, but are the highest ideals, because they are such manifestations of power. In the first place, a man who can work for five days, or for five minutes, without any selfish motive whatever, without thinking of the future, or heaven, or punishment, or anything of the kind, becomes a giant. It is hard to do it, but in the heart of our hearts we know the value of it, and what good it brings. It is the greatest manifestation of power and a tremendous restraint; to restrain is a manifestation of more power than all outgoing action. A carriage with four horses may rush down a hill without restraint;

or the coachman may restrain the horses. Which is the greater manifestation of power, to let them go or to restrain them? A cannon-ball flying through the air goes a long distance and then falls. Another is cut short in its flight by striking against a wall, and intense heat is generated. So, all this outgoing following a selfish motive, goes away; it will not return to you, but if it be restrained it will develop. Restraint will produce a gigantic will, that character which makes a world move. Foolish men do not know the secret; they want to rule mankind. Man does not know that he can rule the whole world if he waits. Let him wait a few years, restrain that foolish idea of governing, and when that idea is wholly gone that man will be a power in the world. But we are such fools! The majority of us cannot see beyond a few years, just as animals cannot see beyond a few steps. Just a little narrow circle; that is our world. We have not the patience to look beyond and thus we become immoral and wicked. It is our weakness, our powerlessness.

But the lowest sorts of work are not to be despised. Let a man who knows no better, work for selfish ends, for name and fame; but a man should always try to get towards the higher motive and to understand what that motive is. Krishna tells us in the Gîtâ, "To work you have the right, but not to the fruits thereof." Leave the fruits alone, leave results alone. Why care for results? When wanting to help a man, never think what that man's attitude should be towards you. Do not care to understand. If you want to do a great or a good work, do not trouble to think what the results will be.

There comes another difficult question with this sort of work. Intense activity is necessary; we must always work. We cannot live a minute without work. What becomes of rest? Here is one side of life-struggle work, to be whirled rapidly round in the current of social life. And here is another picture calm, retiring, everything peaceful around you, very little of noise, only nature.

Neither of them is a perfect picture. If a man goes to live in such a place as soon as he is brought in contact with the surging whirlpool of the world, he will be crushed by it; just as the fish that lives in the deep-sea water, as soon as it is brought to the surface, breaks into pieces; the weight of water on it had kept it together. Can a man who has been used to the turmoil and the rush of life live if he comes into a quiet place? He will suffer and perhaps lose his mind. Very few are able to bear entire solitude. The ideal man is he who in the midst of the greatest silence finds the in tensest activity and in the midst of the in tensest activity finds the silence of the desert. He has learned the secret of restraint; he has controlled himself. He goes through the streets of a big city, with all their traffic, and his mind is as calm as if he were in a cave, where not a sound could reach him, and he is working intensely all the time. That is the ideal of Karma Yoga, and if you have attained to that you have really learned the secret of work.

But we have to begin from the beginning, to take up the works as they come to us and slowly make ourselves more unselfish every day. We must do the work and find out the motive power that is behind, prompting us to the work, and, almost without exception, in the first years, we will find that the motives are always selfish, but gradually this selfishness will melt, by persistence, and at last will come the time when we shall be able to do really unselfish work. We all hope that some time or other, as we struggle through the path of life, there will come a time when we shall become perfectly unselfish, and the moment we attain to that, our powers will be concentrated, and the knowledge which is ours will become manifest.

II. Each Is Great In His Own Place

According to the Sankhya philosophy, nature is composed of three materials, called, in Sanskrit, *Sattva*, *Rajas* and *Tamas*. Tamas is typified as darkness or inactivity: Rajas as activity, where each particle is trying to fly off from the attracting centre, and Sattva is the equilibrium of the two, getting a control of both. Each man is composed of these three materials; in each of us we find that sometimes the Tamas prevails; we become lazy; we cannot move; we are inactive, bound down by certain ideas. At other times activity will prevail, and at still other times that calm control of both will prevail the Sattva. Again, in different men, one of these materials is generally predominant. The characteristic of one man is that of inactivity, dullness and laziness; the characteristic of another man is activity, power, manifestation of energy, and in still another man we find the sweetness, calmness, gentleness, which are controlling both. So, in creation in animals, plants and men we find the typification of all these different materials.

Karma Yoga has specially to deal with these three elements. By teaching us what they are and how to employ them it helps us to do our work better. Human society is a graded organization.

We all know about morality, and we all know about duty, but at the same time we find that in various countries morality differs greatly. What is regarded as moral in one country may in another be considered perfectly immoral. Yet we have the idea that there must be a universal standard of morality. So, it is with duty. The idea of duty varies much among different nations. Two ways are left open to us the way of the ignorant, who think that there is only one way to truth, and that all the rest are wrong, or the way of the wise, who admit that, according to the mental constitution or the different plane of existence in which we are, duty and morality may vary. The important thing is to know that there are gradations of duty and of morality that what is the duty of one state of life in one set of circumstances will not be that of another.

The following example will serve to illustrate: All great teachers have taught "resist not evil" that non-resisting evil is the highest ideal. We all know that if a certain number of us attempted to put that into practice the whole social fabric would fall to pieces, society would be destroyed, the wicked would have possession of our properties and our lives and would do whatever they liked with us. Even if only one day of such non-resistance were practised it would lead to the utter dissolution of society. Yet, intuitively, in our heart of hearts we feel the truth of the teaching, "resist not evil." This seems to us to be the great ideal; yet to teach this doctrine only would be equivalent to condemning a vast proportion of mankind. Not only so, it would be making men feel that they were always doing wrong, cause scruples of conscience in all their actions; it would weaken them, and that constant self-disapproval would breed more vice than any other weakness. To the man who has begun to hate himself the gate to degeneration has been opened, and so with a nation. Our first duty is not to hate ourselves; to advance we must have faith in ourselves first and then in God. He who has no faith in himself can never have faith in God. Therefore, the only alternative remaining to us is to recognize that duty and morality vary under different circumstances; not that the man who resists is doing something wrong, but that in the different circumstances in which he is placed it may become his duty to resist.

In reading the Bhagavad Gîtâ many of you in Western countries may have felt astonished at the second chapter, when Krishna calls Arjuna a hypocrite and a coward because of his refusal to fight or offer resistance on account of his adversaries being his friends and relatives, making the plea that non-resistance was the highest ideal of love. The great lesson to learn is that the two extremes are alike; the extreme positive and the negative are always similar; when the vibrations of light are too slow, we do not see them, nor do we see them when they are too rapid. So, with sound; when very low we do not hear, when very high we do not hear. In like manner is the difference between resistance and non-resistance. One man does not resist because he is weak, lazy, and cannot, and not because he will not; the other is the man who, knowing that he can strike an irresistible blow if he likes, not only does not strike, but blesses his enemies. The one who resists not from weakness commits a sin, and as such will not receive any benefit from his non-resistance, while the other would commit a sin by offering resistance. Buddha gave up his throne and renounced his position; that was true renunciation; but there cannot be any question of renunciation in the case of a beggar who has nothing to renounce. So, we must always take care, when we speak of this non-resistance and ideal love, what we really mean. We must first take care to understand whether we have the power of resistance or not. Then, having the power, if we renounce and do not resist, we are doing a grand act, but if we cannot resist and at the same time try to deceive ourselves that we are actuated by motives of the highest love we are doing the exact opposite. So Arjuna became a coward at the sight of the mighty array against him; his "love" made him forget his duty towards his country and king. That is why Krishna told him that he was a hypocrite: "Thou talkest like a wise man, but thy actions betray thee to be a coward; therefore, stand up and fight!"

Such is the idea of the Karma Yogi. The Karma Yogi is the man who understands that the highest ideal is non-resistance, but who also knows that this is the highest manifestation of power, and that what is called "resisting evil" is but a step on the way towards the manifestation of the highest power, which is non-resistance. Before having attained the highest ideal his duty is to resist; let him work, let him fight, let him strike straight from the shoulder. Then only, when he has gained the power to resist, will non-resistance be a virtue.

Inactivity should be avoided by all means. Activity always means resistance. Resist all evils, mental and physical, and when you have succeeded in resisting, then will calmness come. It is very easy to say, "hate not anybody, resist not any evil," but we know what that means. When the eyes of society are turned towards us, we may make a show of non-resistance, but in our hearts, it is canker all the time. We feel the want of it; we feel that it would be better to resist. If you desire wealth and you know that the whole world will tell you that he who aims at wealth is a very wicked man, you, perhaps, do not dare to plunge into the struggle for wealth, yet at the same time the mind is running day and night after money. This is hypocrisy and will serve no purpose. Plunge into the world, and then, after a time, when you have enjoyed all that is in it, will renunciation come; then will calmness come. So, fulfil your desire for power and everything else, and after you have fulfilled the desire will come the time when you will know that these are very little things; until you have fulfilled this desire, until you have passed through that activity, it is impossible for you to come to that state of calmness and serenity. These ideas of serenity have been preached for thousands of years; everybody born has heard them from childhood, and yet we see very few in the world that have really reached that stage. I do not know if I have seen twenty persons in my life who were really calm and non-resisting, and I have travelled over half the world.

Every man should take up his own ideal and endeavour to accomplish it; that is a surer way than taking up other men's ideals, which he can never hope to accomplish. For instance, we take a child and at once give him the task of walking twenty miles; either the little one dies or one in a thousand may crawl the twenty miles, to reach the end exhausted and half dead. That is what we generally try to do with the world. All men and women, in any society, are not of the same mind, or capacity, and have not the same power to understand things; they must have different ideals, and we have no right to sneer at any ideal. Let everyone do the best he can for his own ideal. I should not be judged by yours or you by mine. The apple tree should not be judged by the standard of the oak nor the oak by that of the apple. To judge the apple tree, you must take the apple standard and for the oak its own standard, and so with all of us.

Unity in variety is the plan of creation. However, men and women may vary individually, there is unity in the background. The different individual characters and classes of men and women are natural variations in the law of creation. Hence, we ought not to judge them by the same standard or put the same ideal before them. Such a course creates only an unnatural struggle, and the result is that man begins to hate himself and is hindered from becoming religious and good. Our duty is to encourage everyone in his struggle to live up to his own highest ideal and strive to make this ideal as near as possible to the truth. In the Hindu morality we find that this fact has been recognized from very ancient times, and in their Scriptures and books on ethics different rules are laid down for the different classes of men, for the householder, the Sannyasin (the man who has renounced the world) and the student.

The life of every individual, according to the Hindu Scriptures, has its peculiar duties apart from what belongs to universal humanity; to each stage of life certain duties are attached by its own nature. No one of these stages of life is superior to the other; the life of the married man is quite as great as that of the man who is not married, but who has devoted himself to religious work. The king on his throne is as great and glorious as the scavenger in the street. Take him off his throne, make him do the work of the scavenger and see how he will fare. Take the scavenger and see how he will rule. It is useless to say that the man who lives out of the world is a greater man than he who lives in the world; it is much more difficult to live in the world and worship God than to give it up and live a free and easy life. The householder marries and carries on his duties as a citizen, while the duties of the man who gives up the world are to devote his energies only to religion. If a man goes out of the world to worship God, he must not think that those who live in the world and work for the good of the world are not worshipping "God; neither must those who live in the world, for wife and children, think that those who give up the world are low vagabonds. Each is great in his own place.

This thought I will illustrate by a story. A certain king used to inquire of all the Sannyâsins that came to his country, "Which is the greater man he who gives up the world and becomes a Sannyâsin, or he who lives in the world and performs his duties as a householder?" Many wise men sought to solve the problem. Some asserted that the Sannyâsin was greater, upon which the king demanded that they prove their assertion. When they could not, he ordered them to marry and become householders. Then others came and said, "The householder who performs his duties is the greater man." Of them, too, the king demanded proofs. When they could not give them, he made them also settle down as householders.

At last, there came a young Sannyâsin, and the king inquired of him. He answered, "Each, O king, is equally great in his place." "Prove this to me," replied the king. "I will prove it to you," said the Sannyâsin, "but you must first come and live as I do for a few days, that I may be able to prove to you what I say." The king consented and followed the Sannyâsin out of his own territory and passed through many territories, until they came to another kingdom. In the capital of that kingdom a great ceremony was going on. The king and the Sannyâsin heard the noise of drums, and music, and criers; the people were assembled in the streets in gala array, and a great proclamation was being made. The king and the Sannyâsin stood there to see what was going on. The crier was saying that the princess, daughter of the king of that country, was about to choose a husband from among those assembled before her.

It was an old custom in India for princesses to choose husbands in this way, and each one had certain ideas of the sort of man she wanted for a husband; some would have the handsomest man; others would have only the most learned; others would have the richest and so on. The princess, in the most splendid array, was carried on a throne, and the announcement was made by criers that the princess so-and-so was about to choose her husband. Then all the princes of the neighbourhood put on their bravest attire and presented themselves before her. Sometimes they, too, had criers to enumerate their advantages and the reasons why they hoped the princess would choose them. The princess was carried around and looked at them and heard what they had to offer, and if she was not pleased, she said to her bearers, "Move on," and no more notice was taken of the rejected suitors. If, however, the princess was pleased with any one of them she threw a garland upon him, and he became her husband.

The princess of the country to which the king and the Sannyâsin had come was having one of these ceremonies. She was the most beautiful princess in the world, and the husband of the princess would be ruler of the kingdom after her father's death. The idea of this princess was to marry the handsomest man, but she could not find the right one to please her. Several times these meetings had taken place, and yet the princess had not selected anyone. This meeting was the most splendid of all; more people than ever had come to it, and it was a most gorgeous scene. The princess comes in on a throne, and the bearers carry her from place to place. She does not care for anyone, and everyone becomes disappointed that this meeting also is to be broken up without any one being chosen. Just then comes a young man, a Sannyâsin, handsome as if the sun had come down to the earth, and he stands in one corner of the assembly, watching what is going on. The throne with the princess comes near him, and as soon as she sees the beautiful Sannyâsin she stops and throws the garland over him. The young Sannyâsin seizes the garland and throws it off, exclaiming, "What nonsense you mean by that; I am a Sannyâsin. What is marriage to me?" The king of that country thinks that perhaps this man is poor, so does not dare to marry the princess, so he said to him, "With my daughter goes half my kingdom now and the whole kingdom after my death!" and he puts the garland again on the Sannyâsin. The young man threw it off once more, saying, "What nonsense is this? I do not want to marry," and walked quickly away from the assembly.

Now the princess had fallen so much in love with this young man that she said, "I must marry this man, or I shall die," and she went after him to bring him back. Then the other Sannyasin, who had brought the king there, said to the king, "King, let us follow this pair," so they walked after them, but a good distance behind. The young Sannyâsin who had refused to marry the princess walked out into the country for several miles, when he came to a forest and struck into it, and the princess followed him, and the other two followed them. Now the young Sannyâsin was well acquainted with that forest and knew all the intricate passages in it, and suddenly he jumped into one of these and disappeared, and the princess could not discover him. After trying for a long time to find him she sat down under a tree and began to weep, for she did not know the way to get out of the forest again. Then the king and the other Sannyâsin came up to her and said, "Do not weep; we will show you the way out of this forest, but it is too dark for us to find it now. Here is a big tree; let us rest under it, and in the morning, we will go early and show you the road to get out."

Now a little bird and his wife and three little baby birds lived on that tree, in a nest. This little bird looked down and saw the three people under the tree and said to his wife, "My dear, what shall be done; here are some guests in the house, and it is winter, and we have no fire?" So he flew away and got a bit of burning firewood in his beak and dropped it before the guests, and they added fuel to it and made a blazing fire. But the little bird was not satisfied. He said again to his wife, "My dear, what shall we do; there is nothing to give these people to eat, and they are hungry, and we are householders; it is our duty to feed anyone who comes to the house. I must do what I can. I will give them my body." So, he plunged down into the midst of the fire and perished. The guests saw him falling and tried to save him, but he was too quick for them and dashed into the fire and was killed.

The little bird's wife saw what her husband did, and she said, "Here are three persons and only one little bird for them to eat. It is not enough; it is my duty as a wife not to let my husband's effort be in vain; let them have my body also," and she plunged down into the fire and was burned to death. Then the three baby birds, when they saw what was done, and that there was still not enough food for the three guests, said, "Our parents have done what they could and still it is not enough. It is our duty to carry on the work of our parents; let our bodies go, too," and they all dashed down into the fire also. The three people could not eat these birds, and they were amazed at what they saw. Somehow or other they passed the night without food, and in the morning the king and the Sannyâsin showed the princess the way, and she went back to her father.

Then the Sannyâsin said to the king, "King, you have seen that each is great in his own place. If you want to live in the world live like those birds, ready at any moment to sacrifice yourself for others. If you want to renounce the world, be like that young man to whom the most beautiful woman and a kingdom were as nothing. If you want to be a householder hold your life a sacrifice for the welfare of others, and if you choose the life of renunciation do not even see beauty, and money, and power. Each is great in his own place, but the duty of the one is not the duty of the other."

III. The Secret Of Work

Helping others physically, by relieving their physical needs, is indeed great, but the help is greater when the need is greater, and the help is more far-reaching. If a man's wants for an hour can be removed it is helping him indeed, but if his wants can be removed for a year it will be more help to him, and if his wants can be removed forever it is the greatest help that can be given. Spiritual knowledge is the only thing that can remove our miseries forever; any other knowledge satisfies wants only for a time. If the nature of the man be changed, then alone all his wants will vanish forever. It is only with the knowledge of the spirit that the faculty of want is annihilated forever, so helping man spiritually is the highest help that can be given to him; he who gives man spiritual knowledge is the greatest benefactor of mankind, and as such we always find that they were the most powerful of men who have helped man in his spiritual needs, because it is the basis of all other works in life. A spiritually strong and sound man will be strong in every other respect, if he wishes, and until there is spiritual strength in mankind even the physical needs cannot be satisfied. Next to spiritual comes intellectual help; the gift of knowledge is a far higher gift than that of food and clothes: it is higher, even, than giving life to a man, because the real life of man consists of knowledge; ignorance is death, and knowledge is life. Life is of very little value if it is a life in the dark, groping through ignorance and misery. Next in order comes, of course, helping a man physically. So, in considering the helping of others, we must always strive not to commit the mistake of thinking that physical help is the only help that can be given; physical help is the last and the least, because there is no permanent satiation. The misery that I feel when I am hungry is satisfied by eating, but hunger returns again; misery can only cease when I am satisfied beyond all want. Then hunger will not make me miserable; no distress, no misery, no sorrow will be able to move me. So that help which tends to make us strong spiritually is the highest help; next to it comes intellectual help and after that physical help.

The miseries of the World cannot be cured by simply physical help; until man's nature changes these physical needs will always arise, and miseries will be always felt, and no amount of physical help given to the world will cure that misery. The only solution of the problem of all this misery in the world is to make mankind pure. Ignorance is the mother of all the evil and all the misery we see. Let men have light, let them be spiritually strong, and if we can accomplish this, if all mankind becomes pure and spiritually strong and educated, then alone will misery cease in the world and not before then. We may convert every house in the country into a charity asylum; we may fill the lands with hospitals, but the misery will still exist until man's character changes.

We read in the Gîtâ again and again that we must all work incessantly, but all work must be composed of good and evil; we cannot do any work which has not some part of good somewhere; there cannot be any work which will not injure someone somewhere. Every work must necessarily be a mixture of good and evil; yet we are told to work incessantly; the good and evil will both have their results, make their Karma; the good action will entail upon us good effect; the bad action bad effect, but good and bad are both bondages of the soul. The solution reached in the Gîtâ is that if we do not attach ourselves to the work, it will not take any effect on us. We will try to understand what is meant by this "non-attachment" to work.

It is the one central idea in the Gîtâ; work incessantly but be not attached to it. "Samskârâ" can be translated very nearly by the word tendency. Using the simile of a lake for the mind, every ripple, every wave that rises in the mind when it subsides does not die out entirely but leaves a mark and a future possibility of that wave coming out again. This mark, with the possibility of the wave reappearing, is what is called Samskârâ. Each work that we do, each movement of the body, each thought in the mind, is leaving such an impression on the mind stuff, and even when they are not obvious on the surface, these marks are sufficiently strong to work beneath the surface, sub-consciously. What we are each moment is determined by the sum total of these impressions on the mind. What I am just at this moment is the effect of the sum total of these marks, of my past life. This is really what is meant by character; each man's character is determined by the sum total of these impressions. If good impressions prevail, that character becomes good; if bad, that character becomes bad. If a man continuously bears bad words, thinks bad thoughts, does bad actions, his mind will be full of these impressions, or marks, and they, unconsciously, will govern the tendency of his work. In fact, these impressions are always working, and the expression will be evil; that man will be a bad man; he cannot help it; the sum total of these impressions will create the strong motive power for doing bad actions; he will be a machine in the hands of his impressions, and they will force him to do evil. Similarly, if a man thinks good thoughts and does good works the sum total of these impressions will be good, and they, in a similar manner, will force him to do good in spite of himself. When a man has done so much good work and thought so many good thoughts that there is an irresistible tendency in his nature to do good in spite of himself, then, even if he thinks he will do evil, the mind, in the sum total of its tendencies, will not allow him to do so; the tendencies will turn him back; he is at the mercy of his good tendencies. When that is the case that man's character is said to be established.

As the tortoise tucks his feet and head inside of his shell, and you may kill him and break him in pieces, yet they will not come out, even so the character of that man who has control over his centres and organs is established. By this continuous reflex of good thoughts, good impressions moving over the surface of the mind, the tendency becomes strong for good, and the result is that we control the "Indriyas" (the sensory and motor organs). Then alone will the character be established; then alone you get to truth; that man is safe forever; he cannot do any evil; you may throw him anywhere; you may put him in any company; there will be no danger for him. There is a still higher stage than having this good tendency, the desire for liberation. You must remember that freedom of the soul is the goal of all these Yogas, and each one equally leads to the same result. Just by work, men can get where Buddha got by meditation and Christ by prayer. Buddha was a Jnani; Christ was a Bhakta, but the same goal was reached. The difficulty is here. Liberation means entire freedom—freedom from the bondages of good, as well as from the bondages of evil. A golden chain is as much a chain as an iron chain. There is a thorn in my finger, and I use another thorn to take the first thorn out, and when I have taken it out I throw both thorns aside; I have no necessity for keeping the second thorn, because both are thorns, after all. So the bad tendencies are to be counteracted by the good tendencies, and the bad marks of the mind should be conquered by fresh waves of good marks, until those that are evil almost disappear, or are subdued and held in control in one corner of the mind; but after that, the good tendencies have also to be conquered; the "attached" must become "unattached." Work, but let not the action or the thought produce a deep impression on the mind; let the ripple come; let huge actions proceed from the muscles and the brain but let them not make any deep impression on the soul. How can that be done? We see that the impression of any action to which we join ourselves remains.

I may meet hundreds of persons during the day, but I meet one I love, and when I retire at night, I may try to think of all the faces, but that face comes which I met only for one minute, and which I loved, and all the others have vanished. My attachment to this particular person caused a deeper impression on my mind than all the other faces. Physiologically, the impressions have all been the same; every one of these faces that I saw pictured itself on the retina, and the brain took the picture in, and yet there was no similar effect upon the mind. But in the case of that man, of whom I caught, perhaps, only a glimpse, a deeper impression was made, because the other faces found no association in my mind; most of them, perhaps, were entirely new, faces about which I never thought before, but that one face, of which I got only a glimpse, found associations inside. Perhaps I had pictured him for years, knew hundreds of things about him, and this one new thing found hundreds of kindred things inside my mind, and all these associations were aroused; the impression on my mental vision was a hundred times more than the seeing of all those different faces together, and such being the case, a deep impression will be immediately made upon the mind.

Therefore, be "unattached;" let things work; let brain centres work, work incessantly, but let not a ripple conquer the mind. Work as if you were a stranger in this land, a sojourner; work incessantly, but do not bind yourselves; bondage is terrible. This world is not our habitation, it is only one of the many stages through which we are passing. Remember that great saying of the Sankhya Philosophy, "The whole of nature is for the soul, not the soul for nature." The very reason of nature's existence is for the education of the soul; it has no other meaning; it is there because the soul must have knowledge, and through knowledge will free itself. If we remember this always, we shall never be attached to nature; we shall know that nature is a book in which we are to read, and when we have gained that knowledge the book itself ceases to be of value to us. Instead of that, however, we are identifying ourselves with nature; we are thinking that the soul is for nature, just as the common saying is that one man "lives to eat" and another "eats to live;" we are continually making this mistake; we are regarding nature as ourselves and are becoming attached to it, and as soon as this attachment comes there is this deep impression on the soul, which binds us down and makes us work like slaves.

The whole gist of this teaching is that you should work like a master and not as a slave; work incessantly, but not slave's work. Do you not see how everybody works? Nobody can rest; ninety-nine per cent of mankind work as slaves, and the result is misery; it is selfish work. Work through freedom! Work through love! The word love is very difficult to understand; it never comes until there is freedom. There is no love in the slave. If you buy a slave and tie him down in chains and make him work for you he will work like a drudge, but there will be no love. So when we ourselves work for the world as slaves, there is no love, and it is not true work. The same applies to our work for our relatives and friends, even for our own selves. Suppose a man loves a woman; he wishes to have her all to himself and feels extremely jealous about her every moment; he wants her to sit near him, to stand near him and eat and move at his bidding. He is a slave to her. That is not love; it is a sort of morbid affection of the slave, insinuating itself as love. It cannot be love, because it is painful; if she does not do what he wants it brings pain. With love there is no painful reaction; love only brings a reaction of bliss; if it does not it is not love; we are mistaking something else for love. When you have succeeded in loving your husband, your wife, your children, the whole world, the universe, in such a manner that there is no reaction of pain, or jealousy, no selfish feeling, then you are in a fit state to be unattached.

Krishna says, "Look at me, Arjuna! If I stop from work for one moment the whole universe will die. Yet I have nothing to gain from the universe, I am one Lord. I have nothing to gain from the universe; but why do I work? Because I love the world." God is unattached because He loves; that real love makes us unattached. Wherever there is this attachment, this tremendous clinging, you must know it is physical, a sort of physical attraction between particles of matter and other particles of matter, something that attracts two bodies nearer and nearer all the time, and if they cannot get near it becomes painful; but where there is real love it does not count on physical attachment at all. That body may be a thousand miles distant; love is all the same; it does not die; there will never be a painful reaction.

To attain this non-attachment is almost a life work, but as soon as we have reached this point, we have attained the goal and become free. The bondage of nature falls from us, and we see nature as it is; she forges no more chains for us. We stand entirely free and take not the results of work into consideration. Why care what may be the results, either good or bad? The man who works through freedom does not care for the results. Do you ask anything from your children in return for what you have given them? It is your duty to work for them, and there it stops. Whatever you do for a particular person, a city, or a State, do it, but assume the same attitude as you have towards your children—expect nothing. If you can incessantly take that position that you are a giver, that everything given by you is a free offering to the world, without any thought of return, that will be work which will not bring attachment. Attachment only comes when we expect something.

This idea of complete self-sacrifice is illustrated in the following story: After the battle of Kurukshetra the five Pându brothers held a great sacrifice and made very large gifts to the poor. All the people expressed amazement at the greatness and richness of the sacrifice and said that such a sacrifice the world had never seen before. But, after the ceremony, there came a little mongoose; half his body was golden, and the other half was brown, and he began to roll himself on the floor of the sacrificial hall. Then he said to those around, "You are all liars; this is no sacrifice." "What!" they exclaimed, "you say this is no sacrifice! Do you not know how money and jewels were poured out upon the poor and everyone became rich and happy? This was the most wonderful sacrifice any man ever made." But the mongoose said, "There was once a little village, and in it there dwelt a poor Brahmin, with his wife, his son and his son's wife. They were very poor and lived on alms gained in preaching and teaching, for which men made little gifts to them.

"There came in that land a three years' famine, and the poor Brahmin suffered more than ever. At last for five days the family starved, but on the fifth day the father brought home a little barley flour, which he had been fortunate enough to find, and he divided it into four parts, one for each of them. They prepared it for their meal, and just as they were about to eat it a knock came at the door. The father opened it, and there stood a guest. In India a guest is sacred; he is as a god for the time being, and must be treated as such. So the poor Brahmin said, 'Come in, sir; you are welcome.' He set before the guest his own portion of food, and the latter quickly ate it up and then said, 'Oh, sir, you have killed me; I have been starving for ten days, and this little bit has but increased my hunger.' Then the wife said to her husband, 'Give him my share,' but the husband said, 'Not so.' The wife, however, insisted, saying, 'Here is a poor man, and it is our duty as householders to see that he is fed, and it is my duty as a wife to give him my portion, seeing that you have no more to offer him.' Then she gave her share to the guest; and he ate it up and said he was still burning with hunger. So, the son said, 'Take my portion also; it is the duty of a son to help his father to fulfil his obligations.' The guest ate that, but remained still unsatisfied; so, the son's wife gave him her portion also. That was sufficient, and the guest departed, blessing them.

"That night those four people died of starvation. A few grains of that flour had fallen on the floor, and when I rolled my body on them half of it became golden, as you see it. Since then, I have been all over the world, hoping to find another sacrifice like that, but never have I found one; nowhere else has the other half of my body been turned into gold. That is why I say this is no sacrifice."

IV. What is Duty?

It is necessary to know what work is, and with that comes, naturally, the question, "What is duty?" If I have to do something I must first know my duty, and then I can do it. The idea of duty, again, is very different in different nations. The Mohammedan says what is written in his book, the Qur'ân, is his duty; the Hindu says what is in his book, the Vedas, is his duty, and the Christian says what is in his Bible is his duty. So, we find that there must be varied ideas of duty, differing according to different states in life, different periods, and different nations. The term "duty," like every other universal abstract term, is impossible to define; we can only get an idea of it by describing the surroundings and by knowing its actions and its results. To make an objective definition of duty would be entirely impossible; there is no such thing as objective duty. Yet there is duty from the subjective side. Any action that makes us go godward is a good action and is our duty; any action that makes us go downward is an evil action. There is only one idea which is universal for all mankind, of any age, sect or country, and that has been summed up in the Sanskrit aphorism: "Do not injure any being; non-injuring any being is virtue; injuring any being is vice."

One point we ought to remember is that we should always

try to see the duty of others through their eyes, and never judge the customs of other races or other peoples by our own standard. This is the great lesson to learn. "I am not the standard of the universe. I have to accommodate myself to the world, and not the world to me." Therefore, we see that environments will change our duties, and doing in the best way that duty which is ours at a certain time is the best thing we can do in this world. Let us do that duty, which is ours by birth, and when we have done that do the duty which is ours by our position. Each man is placed in some position in life and must do the duties of that position first. There is one great difficulty in human nature, that man never looks at himself. He thinks he is quite as fit to be on the throne as the king. Even if he is, he must first show that he has done the duty of his own position, and when he has done that, higher duty will come to him.

Later on, we will find that even the idea of duty will have to be changed, and that the greatest work is only done when there is the least motive urging us from behind. Yet it is work through duty that leads us to work without any idea of duty; when work will become worship nay, higher, work will stand alone for its own sake. But that is the ideal, and the way lies through duty. We shall find the philosophy behind all duties, either in the form of ethics or love, is the same as that in every other Yoga attenuating the lower self, so that the real Self may shine; to circumscribe the frittering away of energies on the lower planes of existence, so that the soul may manifest itself on the higher planes. This is accomplished by the continuous denial of low desires, a denial which duty rigorously requires. The whole organization of society has thus been developed, consciously or unconsciously, as the land of actions, the field of experience, where, by limiting the desires of selfishness, we open the way to an unlimited expansion of the real nature of man.

Duty is seldom sweet. It is only when love oils its wheels that it runs smoothly; else it is a continuous friction. What parents can do their duties to their children? What children to their parents? What husband to his wife? What wife to her husband? Do we not meet with cases of friction every day in our lives? Duty is sweet only through love, love shines alone in freedom; yet is it freedom to be a slave to the senses, to anger, to jealousies and a hundred other petty things that must occur every day in human life? In all these little roughness's that we meet with in life the highest expression of freedom is to forbear. Women, slaves to their own irritable, jealous tempers, are apt to attribute the blame to their husbands, and assert their freedom, as they think, not knowing that they are only proving that they are slaves. So, with husbands who are continually finding fault with their wives.

Chastity is the first virtue in man or woman, and the man who, however he may have strayed away, cannot be brought to the right path by a gentle and loving and chaste wife, is indeed very rare. This world is not yet as bad as that. We hear much about brutal husbands all over the world and the impurity of men, but it is true that there are quite as many brutal and impure women as men. If all women were as good and pure as their own constant assertions would lead people to believe, I am perfectly satisfied that there would not be one impure man in the world. With whom could men become impure? What brutality is there which purity and chastity cannot conquer? A good, chaste wife, who thinks of every other man except her own husband as her child and has the attitude of a mother toward all men, will grow so great in the power of purity that there will not be a single man, however brutal, who will not feel an atmosphere of holiness in her presence. Similarly, every husband must look upon all women, except his own wife, in the light of his own mother or daughter or sister. That man, again, who wants to be a teacher of religion must look upon every woman as his mother, and always behave toward her as such.

The position of the mother is the highest in the world, as it is the one place in which to learn and exercise the greatest unselfishness. The love of God is the only love that is higher than mother's love; all others are lower. It is the duty of the mother to think of her children first and then of herself. But, instead of that, if the parents are always thinking of themselves first, the result is that the relation between parents and children becomes as the relation between the birds and their offspring, who, as soon as they are fledged, cease to recognize any parents. Blessed, indeed, is the man who is able to look upon woman as the representative of the Motherhood of God. Blessed, indeed, is the woman to whom man represents the Fatherhood of God. Blessed are the children who look upon their parents as Divinity manifested on earth.

The only way to rise spiritually is by doing the duty that is in our hands now, and making ourselves stronger and going higher, until we reach the highest state. Nor is duty to be slighted. A man who does the lower work is not, therefore, a lower man than he who does the higher work. A man should not be judged by the nature of his duties, but by the manner in which he does them. His manner of doing them and power to do them is the test of a man. A shoemaker who can turn out a strong, well-made pair of shoes in the shortest time is a better man according to his works than a would-be professor who talks nonsense every day of his life.

A certain young Sannyâsin went to a forest and there meditated and worshipped and practised Yoga for a long time. After twelve years of hard work and practice, he was one day sitting under a tree, when some dry leaves fell upon his head. He looked up and saw a crow and a crane fighting on the top of the tree, and they made him very angry. He said: "What! You dare throw those dry leaves upon my head!" and as he looked upon them with anger, a flash of fire burst from his head the

Yogi's power and burnt the birds to ashes. He was very glad; he was almost overjoyed at this development of power; he could burn, at a glance, the crow and the crane. After a time, he had to go into the town to beg his bread. He came and stood at a door and said: "Mother, give me food." A voice came from inside the house: "Wait a little, my son." The young man thought: "You wretched woman, dare you make me wait! You do not know my power yet." While he was thinking this the voice came again: "Boy, don't be thinking too much of yourself. Here is neither crow nor crane." He was astonished; still he had to wait. At last, a woman came, and he fell at her feet and said: "Mother, how did you know that?" She said: "My boy, I do not know your Yoga or your practices. I am a common, everyday woman, but I made you wait because my husband is ill, and I was nursing him, and that was my duty. All my life I have struggled to do my duty. As a daughter, when I was unmarried, I did my duty, and now, when I am married, I still do my duty; that is all the Yoga I practise, and by doing my duty I have become illumined; thus, I could read your thoughts and know what you had done in the forest. But if you want to know something higher than this, go to such and such a town and to the market, and there you will find a butcher, and he will tell you something that you will be very glad to learn." The Sannyâsin thought: "Why go to that town and to a butcher." (Butchers are the lowest class in our country; they are called Chandâlas; they are not touched because they are butchers; they do the duty of scavengers, and so forth.)

But after what he had seen his mind was opened a little, so he went, and when he came to the city he found the market, and there saw, at a distance, a big, fat butcher slashing away at animals, with big knives, and bargaining with different people. The young man said, "Lord, help me, is this the man from whom I am going to learn? He is the incarnation of a demon if he is anything." In the meantime, this man looked up and said, "Swâmi, did that lady send you here? Take a seat until I have finished my business." The Sannyâsin thought, "What comes to me here?" but he took a seat, and the man went on, and after he had finished all his selling and buying, took his money and said to the Sannyâsin, "Come here, sir; come to my home."

So, they went there, and the butcher gave him a seat and said, "Wait there." Then he went into the house and there were his father and mother. He washed them and fed them and did all he could to please them, and then came and took a seat before the Sannyâsin and said, "Now, sir, you are come here to see me; what can I do for you?" Then this great Sannyâsin asked him a few questions about the soul and God, and this butcher gave him a lecture which is a very celebrated book in India, the "Vyâdha Gîtâ," and is to be found in the Mahâbhârata, the great Indian epic. It is one of the highest flights in the Vedanta, the highest flight of metaphysics. You have heard of the Bhagavad Gîtâ, Krishna's sermon. When you have finished that you should read the "Vyâdha Gîtâ," it is an epitome of Vedânta philosophy. When the butcher had finished the Sannyâsin was astonished. He said, "Why are you in that body, with such knowledge as yours? Why are you in a butcher's body, and doing such filthy, ugly work?" "My son," replied the Chandâla, "no duty is ugly, and no duty is impure. My birth placed me in these circumstances and environments. In my boyhood I learned the trade; I am unattached, and I try to do my duty well. I try to do my duty as a householder, and I try to do all I can to make my father and mother happy. I neither know your Yoga, nor have become a Sannyâsin; never went out of the world, nor into a forest, but all this has come to me through doing my duty in my position."

There is a sage in India, a great Yogi, one of the most wonderful men I have seen in my life. He is a peculiar man; he will not teach anyone; if you ask him a question he will not answer. It is too much for him to take the position of a teacher; he will not take it. If you ask a question, and if you wait for some days, in the course of conversation, he will bring the subject out himself, and wonderful light he will throw on it. He told me once the secret of work, and what he said was, "Let the end and the means be joined into one, and that is the secret of work." When you are doing work, do not think of anything beyond. Do it as worship, and the highest worship, and devote your whole life to it for the time being. Thus, in this story, the butcher and the woman did their duty with cheerfulness, and wholeheartedness, and willingness, and the result was that they became illuminated, clearly showing that the right performance of the duties of any station, and being non-attached, lead to the highest realization.

V. We Help Ourselves, Not The World

Our duty to others means helping others, doing good to the world. Why should we do good to the world? Apparently to help the world, but really to help ourselves. We should always try to help the world; that should be the highest motive power in us; but, when we analyse it properly, we shall find that this world does not require our help. This world was not made that you or I should come and help it. I once read a sermon in which was said: "All this beautiful world is very good because it gives us time and opportunity to help others." Apparently, it was a very beautiful sentiment, but, in one sense, it was a curse, for is it not a blasphemy to say that the world needs our help? We cannot deny that there is much misery in it; to go out and help others is, therefore, the highest motive power we have, although, in the long run, we shall find that it is only helping ourselves. As a boy I had some white mice. They were kept in a little box and had little wheels made for them, and when the mice tried to cross the wheels, the wheels turned and turned, and the mice never got anywhere. So, with the world and our helping it. The only help is, that you get exercise. This world is neither good nor evil; each man manufactures a world for himself. If a blind man begins to think of it, it is either as soft or hard, or cold or hot. We are a mass of happiness or misery; we have seen that hundreds of times in our lives. As a rule, the young are optimistic and the old pessimistic. The young have all life before them, and the old are complaining that their day is gone. Hundreds of desires, which they cannot fulfil, are struggling in their brains. Life is at an end for them. Both are foolish. This life is neither good nor evil. It is according to the different states of mind in which we look at the world. The most intelligent man would call it neither good nor evil. Fire, by itself, is neither good nor evil. When it keeps us warm, we say: "How beautiful is fire!" When it burns our fingers, we blame the fire. Still, it was neither good nor bad. As we use it, it produces that feeling of good or bad, and so is this world. It is perfect. By perfection is meant that it is perfectly fitted to meet its ends. We can all be perfectly sure that it will go on, and that it does not need any help from us.

Yet we must do good. It is the highest motive power we have, knowing all the time it is a privilege to help. Do not stand on a pedestal and take five cents and say, "Here, my poor man," but be grateful that the poor man is there, so that by giving to him you are able to help yourself. It is not the receiver that is blessed, but the giver. Be thankful that you are allowed to exercise your power of benevolence and mercy in the world, and thus become pure and perfect. All good acts tend to make us pure and perfect. What can we do at best? Build a hospital, make roads, or erect charity asylums! We may organize a charity and collect two or three millions of dollars, build a hospital with one million, with the second give balls and drink champagne, and of the third let the officers steal half, and the rest may finally reach the poor, but what are these? One mighty wind, in five minutes, can break it all up. What shall we do then? One volcanic eruption can sweep away all our roads, and hospitals, and cities and buildings. Let us give up all this foolish talk of doing good to the world. It is not waiting for your or my help, yet we must work and constantly do good, because it is a blessing to ourselves. That is the only way we can become perfect. No beggar ever owed a single cent to us, we owe everything to him, because he has allowed us to exercise our powers of pity and charity on him. It is entirely wrong to think that we have done, or can do good to the world, or have helped such and such people. It is a foolish thought, and all foolish thoughts bring misery. We think we have helped someone and expect him to thank us, and, because he does not, unhappiness comes to us. Why expect anything? If we were really unattached, we should escape all this pain of vain expectation, and could do good work in the world. Never will unhappiness or misery come through work done without attachment. This world will go on with its happiness and misery through eternity.

There was a poor man who wanted some money, and, somehow, he had heard that if he could get hold of a ghost or some spirit, he could command him to bring money or anything he liked; so, he was very anxious to get hold of a ghost. He went about searching for a man who would give him a ghost, and at last he found a sage, with great powers, and besought this sage to help him. The sage asked him what he would do with a ghost. "I want a ghost to work for me; teach me how to get hold of one, sir, I desire it very much," replied the man. But the sage said, "Don't disturb yourself, go home." The next day the man went again to the sage and began to weep and pray. "Give me a ghost; I must have a ghost, sir, to help me!" At last, the sage was disgusted, and said, "Take this charm, repeat this magic word, and a ghost will come, and whatever you say to this ghost he will do. But beware; they are terrible beings and must be kept continually busy. If you fail to give him work, he will take your life." The man replied: "That's easy; I can give him work for all his life." Then he went to a forest, and after long repetition of the magic word, a huge ghost appeared before him, with big teeth, and said: "I am a ghost. I have been conquered by your magic.

But you must keep me constantly employed. The moment you stop I will kill you." The man said: "Build me a palace," and the ghost said, "It is done; the palace is built!' "Bring me money," said the man. "Here is your money," said the ghost. "Cut this forest down and build a city in its place." "That is done," said the ghost; "anything more?" Now the man began to be frightened and said: "I can give him nothing more to do; he does everything in a trice." The ghost said: "Give me something to do or I will eat you up." The poor man could find no further occupation for him and was frightened. So, he ran and ran and at last reached the sage, and said: "Oh, sir, protect my life!" The sage asked him what was the matter, and the man replied: "I have nothing to give the ghost to do. Everything I tell him to do he does in a moment, and he threatens to eat me up if I do not give him work." Just then the ghost arrived, saying, "I'll eat you up; I'll eat you up," and he would have swallowed the man. The man began to shake and begged the sage to save his life. The sage said: "I will find you a way out. Look at that dog with a curly tail. Draw your sword quickly and cut the tail off and give it to the ghost to straighten out." The man cut off the dog's tail and gave it to the ghost, saying, "Straighten that out for me." The ghost took it and slowly and carefully straightened it out, but as soon as he let go, it instantly curled up again. Once more he laboriously straightened it out, only to find it again curled up as soon as he attempted to let go of it. Again, he patiently straightened it out, but as soon as he let it go, it curled up once more. So, he went on for days and days, until he was exhausted, and said, "I was never in such trouble before in my life. I am an old veteran ghost, but never before was I in such trouble. I will make compromise with you," he said to the man. "You let me off and I will let you keep all I have given you and will promise not to harm you." The man was much pleased and accepted the offer gladly.

This world is that dog's curly tail, and people have been striving to straighten it out for hundreds of years, but when they let go, it curls up again. How can it be otherwise? One must first know how to work without attachment, then he will not be a fanatic. When we know that this world is like a dog's curly tail and will never straighten, we shall not become fanatics. They can never do real work. If there were no fanaticism in the world it would make much more progress than it does now. It is all silly nonsense to think that fanaticism makes for the progress of mankind. On the contrary, it is a retarding element, creating hatred and anger, causing people to fight each other, and making them unsympathetic. Whatever we think and believe we consider the best in the world, and what we do not believe, we regard as of no value. So, always remember this curly tail of the dog whenever you have a tendency to become a fanatic. You need not worry or make yourself sleepless; the world will go on. When you have avoided fanaticism then alone will you work well. It is the level-headed man, the calm man of good judgment and cool nerves, of great sympathy and love, who does good work. The fanatic has no sympathy.

VI. Non-Attachment Is Complete Self-Abnegation

Just as every action that emanates from us comes back to us, even so our actions may act on other people and theirs on us. Perhaps all of you have observed it as a fact that when persons do evil actions, they become more and more evil, and when they begin to do good, they become stronger and stronger and do good all the time. This multiplication of action cannot be explained on any other ground, except that we can act and react upon each other. To take a simile from physical science, when I am doing a certain action, my mind is in a certain form of vibration; all minds under similar circumstances would have the tendency to be affected by my mind. If there are different musical instruments in one room all of you have noticed that if one is struck the others have a tendency to vibrate the same note. So, taking this as an illustration, it shows that the instruments had each the same tension and would be affected alike by the same impulse. So, all minds that have the same tension will be equally affected by the same thought. Of course, it will vary, according to the distance, but it will be open to be affected. Suppose I am doing an evil act, my mind is in a certain state of vibration, and all minds in the universe, in the similar state, will have the possibility of being affected by my mind. So, when I am doing a good action, my mind has another state of tension, and all minds similarly attuned will have the possibility of being affected, and this power of affection will be more or less according to the tension.

Following this simile further, it is quite possible that, just as light waves may travel for millions of years before they reach their object, so these thought waves may travel hundreds of years, until they meet with an object with which they vibrate in unison. It is quite possible, therefore, that this atmosphere of ours is full of such thought pulsations, both good and evil. Every thought projected from every brain goes on pulsating, as it were, until it meets an object. Any mind which is opening itself to receive some of these will receive them immediately. So, when a man is doing evil action, he has brought his mind to a certain state of tension, and all the waves corresponding to that state of tension, which are already in the atmosphere, will struggle to enter his mind. That is why an evildoer generally goes on doing more and more evil. His action is intensified. Such, also, will be the case with the doer of good; he will open himself to all the good waves that are in the atmosphere, and his good actions will be intensified. We run, therefore, a twofold danger in doing evil; first, we open ourselves to all the evil influences surrounding us; secondly, we create evil which will affect others. It may be possible that our evil actions will affect others hundreds of years hence. In doing evil we injure ourselves and others also. In doing good we do good to ourselves and to others, and, like all other forces in man, these good and evil forces gather strength from outside.

According to Karma Yoga, the action one has done cannot be destroyed until it has borne fruit; no power in nature can stop it from bearing its results. If I do an evil action, I must suffer for it; there is no power in this universe to stop or stay it. So, if I do a good action there is no power in the universe which can stop its bearing good results. The cause must have its effect; nothing can restrain it. Now comes a very fine and serious question about Karma Yoga that these actions of ours, either good or evil, are intimately connected with each other. We cannot put a line of demarcation and say this action is entirely good and this entirely evil. There is no action which does not bear good and evil at the same time. To take the nearest example: I am talking to you, and some of you, perhaps, think I am doing good, and at the same time I am, perhaps, killing thousands of microbes in the atmosphere; I am doing evil to something else. When it is very near to us and affects those, we know we say it is very good action, if it affects them in a good manner. For instance, you may call my speaking to you very good, but the microbes will not; the microbes you do not see, but yourselves you do see. The effect on you is obvious, but that on the microbes is not obvious. And so, if we analyse our evil actions, we will find that some good was done somewhere. "He who in good action sees that there is something evil in it and who in the midst of evil sees that there is some good in it somewhere has known the secret of work."

But what follows from it? That, however, we may try, there cannot be any action which is perfectly pure, or any which is perfectly impure, taking purity or impurity in the sense of injury or non-injury. We cannot breathe or live without injuring others, and every bit of food we eat is taken from another's mouth; our very lives are crowding out some other lives. It may be men, or animals, or small microbes, but someone we have to crowd out. That being the case, it naturally follows that perfection can never be attained by work. We may work through all eternity, but there will be no way out of this intricate maze; you may work on, and on, and on; there will be no end.

The second point to consider is, what is the end of work? We find the vast majority of people in every country believing that there will be a time when this world will become perfect, when there will be no disease, nor death, nor unhappiness, nor wickedness. That is a very good idea, a very good motive power for the ignorant, but if we think for a moment, we will find that on the very face of it it cannot be so. How can it be, seeing that good and bad are the obverse and reverse of the same coin? How can you have good without evil at the same time? What is meant by perfection? A perfect life is a contradiction in terms. Life itself is a state of continuous struggle between ourselves and everything outside. Every moment we are fighting with external nature, and if we are defeated our life will have to go. It is a continuous struggle for food. If food fails, we die. Life is not a simple effect, but a compound effect. This compound struggle between something inside and the external world is what we call life. So, on the very face of it, when this struggle ceases, there will be an end of what we call life.

What is meant by this ideal happiness is that this struggle will cease altogether. But then life will cease, for the struggle can only cease when life has ceased. Then, again, before we have attained to one-thousandth part of it, this earth will have cooled down, and we will not be. So, this millennium cannot be in this world, if it can be anywhere else. Every act of charity, every thought of sympathy, every action of help, every good deed, is taking so much away from our little selves and making us think of ourselves the least and, therefore, is good. Here we find that the Jnani, or Bhakta, or Karmi, all come to one point. The highest ideal is eternal and entire self-abnegation, where there is no "I," but is all thou; and consciously, or unconsciously, Karma Yoga leads to that. It is the basis of all morality; you may extend it to men, or animals, or angels, but it is the one basic idea, the one fundamental principle running through all ethical systems.

You will find various classes of men in this world. First, there are the God-men, who are abnegating themselves entirely and will do good to others, even at the sacrifice of their own lives. These are the highest of men. If there are a hundred of such in any country, that country need not despair. Then there are good men, who do good to others so long as it does not injure themselves; and there is a third class, who, to do good to themselves, would injure others. It is said there is a fourth class of people, who will injure others for injury's sake. Just as there are at one pole of existence the good men, who will do good for god's sake, so, at the other pole, there are others who will injure others, just for the sake of injury. They do not gain anything thereby, but it is their nature. So, we see that the man who sacrifices himself to do good to others, the man with the highest self-abnegation, is the greatest man.

Here are two Sanskrit words. One is called "Pravritti," revolving towards, and the other is "Nivritti," revolving away. The "revolving towards" is what we call the world, "I and mine," those who are always enriching that "me" by wealth, and property, by power, and name, and fame, always wanting to accumulate everything towards one centre, and that centre "myself." That is the "pravritti," the natural tendency of every human being; taking everything from everywhere and heaping it around one centre, and that centre his own sweet self. When this begins to break, when it is "nivritti," "going away from," then begin morality and religion. Both "pravritti" and "nivritti" are work, but one is evil work, and the other is good work. This "nivritti" is the basis of all morality and all religion, and the very perfection of it is entire self-abnegation, readiness to sacrifice mind, body and everything for another being. When a man has reached that state, he has attained to the perfection of Karma Yoga. This is the highest result of good works. If a man has not studied a single philosophy, if he does not believe in any God, and never has, if he has never prayed even once in his whole life, but, if the simple power of good actions has brought him to that state where he is ready to give up his life and all else for others, he has arrived at the same point to which the religious man will come through his prayers and the philosopher through his knowledge, and so you find that the philosopher, the worker, and the devotee, all meet at one point, and that one point is self-abnegation. However, the systems of philosophy may differ in opinion, all mankind stands in reverence and awe before the man who is ready to sacrifice himself for others. No more question of creed, or doctrine even men who are very much opposed to all religious ideas, when they see one of these acts of complete self-sacrifice, must revere it. Have you not seen even a most bigoted Christian, when he reads Sir Edwin Arnold's "Light of Asia," stand in reverence for Buddha, who preached no God, preached nothing but self-sacrifice? The only thing is that the bigot does not know that his own aim and end in life is exactly the same. The worshipper, by keeping constant the idea of God and a surrounding of good, comes to the same point at last, "Thy will be done," and keeps nothing for himself. That is self-abnegation. The philosopher, with his knowledge, sees that the seeming self is a delusion and easily gives it up; yet it is self-abnegation. So, the paths of Karma, Bhakti and Jnana all meet here, and this is what was meant by all the great preachers of ancient times, when they taught that God is not the world. There is one thing which is world and another which is God, and this is very true; what they mean by the world is selfishness. Unselfishness is God. One may live on a throne, in a golden palace, and be perfectly unselfish, and he is in God. Another may live in a hut, and wear rags, and have nothing in the world, yet, if he is selfish, he is intensely merged in the world.

To come back to one of our points, we say that we cannot do good without doing some evil, or evil without doing some good. Knowing this, how can we work? A solution is found in the Gîtâ, the theory of non-attachment, to be attached to nothing.

Know that you are separated entirely from this world; that you are in the world, but whatever you are doing, you are not doing for your own sake. Any action that you do for yourself will bring an effect on you. If it is a good action you will have to take the good effect, and, if bad, you will have to take the bad effect; but any action that is not done for your own sake, whatever it be, will have no effect on you. Even if a man kill the whole world, he is neither killed nor is killing, when he knows that he is not acting for himself at all. Therefore, Karma Yoga teaches, do not give up the world; live in the world, take it in as much as you can, but not for the sake of enjoyment. Enjoyment should not be the goal. First kill yourself and then take the whole world as yourself. "The old man must die." This old man is this selfish idea that the whole world is made for our enjoyment. There are people who teach us that all the animals were created for us to kill and eat, and that this universe is for the enjoyment of man. That is all foolishness. A tiger might as well say, "Man was created for me," and cry, "O Lord, how wicked are these men, who do not come and put themselves before us to be eaten; they are breaking your law." If the world is created for us, we are also created for the world. That this world is created for our enjoyment is the idea that holds us down. This world is not for our sake; millions pass out of it every year; the world does not feel it; millions of others have been supplied. Just as the world is for us, we are for the world.

To work, therefore, first give up the idea of attachment. Secondly, do not mix in the fray; hold yourself as a witness and go on working. A sage has said, "Look upon your children as your nurse does." The nurse will take your baby and fondle it and play with it and behave as gently as if it were her own child, but as soon as you give her notice she is ready to start off with her baggage from the house. Everything is forgotten; it would not give the ordinary nurse the least pang to leave your children and take up other children. Even so be with your own.

You are the nurse, and, if you believe in God, believe that these are all His. The greatest weakness generally insinuates itself as the greatest good and strength. This is weakness to think that someone depends on me, and I can do good to somebody. This pride is the mother of all our attachment, and through this attachment comes all our pain. We must inform our minds that no one in this universe depends upon us; not one beggar depends on our charity; not one soul on our kindness; not one on our help. They are all helped and will be helped if millions of us were not here. The course of nature will not stop for you and me; it is only a blessed privilege to you and me that we are allowed in the shape of help to others, to educate ourselves. This is one lesson to learn, through the whole of our lives, and when we have learned it fully, we shall never be unhappy; we can go and mix anywhere and everywhere. This very year some of our friends may have died. Is the world waiting for them? Is its current stopped? It goes on. So, drive out, thrash out of your mind, this idea that you have to do something for the world; the world does not require any help from you. When you have trained your nerves and your muscles to this idea there will be no reaction in the form of pain. When you give something to a man and expect nothing do not expect the man to be grateful it will not tell upon you, because you never expected anything, never thought you had a right to anything; you gave what he deserved; his own Karma got it for him; your Karma made you the carrier. Why should you be proud of giving something? You are the porter who carried the money, and the world deserved it by its own Karma. Where is the reason for pride? There is nothing very great in what you give to the world. When you have got the feeling of non-attachment there will be neither good nor evil work for you. It is only selfishness that makes the difference of good and evil. It is a very hard thing to understand; but you will come to learn in time that nothing in the universe has power over you until you admit it. Nothing has power over the Self of man until the self becomes a fool and obeys the power. So, by non-attachment, you deny the power of anything to act upon you. It is very easy to say that nothing has the right to act upon you until you allow it, but what is the sign of the man who really does not allow anything to work upon him, who is neither happy nor unhappy, when he is acted upon by the external world? The sign is that it makes no change in his mind; in good fortune or in ill he remains the same.

There was a great sage called Vyâsa. This Vyâsa was the writer of the Vedânta philosophy, a holy man. His father had tried to become a very perfect man and failed; his grandfather tried, failed. His great-grandfather tried, failed. He himself did not succeed perfectly, but his son, Shuka, was born perfect. He taught this son, and, after teaching him himself, he sent him to the court of King Janaka. There was a great king called Janaka Videha. Videha means "outside the body." Although a king, he had entirely forgotten that he was a body; he was a spirit all the time. This boy was sent to be taught by him. The King knew that Vyâsa's son was coming to him to learn, so he made certain arrangements beforehand, and when this boy presented himself at the gates of the palace the guards took no notice of him whatsoever. They only gave him a place to sit, and he sat there for "three days and nights, nobody speaking to him, nobody asking who he was or whence he was. He was the son of this great sage; his father was honoured by the whole country, and he himself was a most respected person, yet the low, vulgar guards of the palace would take no notice of him. After that, suddenly, the ministers of the King and all the high officials came there and received him with the greatest honours. They took him in and showed him into splendid rooms, gave him the most fragrant baths and wonderful dresses, and for eight days they kept him there in all kinds of luxury. That face did not change; he was the same in the midst of this luxury as at the door. Then he was brought before the King. The King was on his throne, music was playing, and dancing and other amusements going on. The King gave him a cup of milk, full to the brim, and asked him to go seven times round the hall without spilling a drop. The boy took the cup and proceeded in the midst of this music and the beautiful faces. Seven times he went round, and not a drop of milk was spilled; The boy's mind could not be attracted by anything in the world, unless he allowed it. And when he brought the cup to the King, the King said to him, "What your father has taught you and what you have learned yourself I can only repeat; you have known the truth; go home."

Thus, the man that has practised control over himself cannot be acted upon by anything outside; there is no more slavery for him. The mind has become free; such a man alone is fit to live in the world. We generally find men of two opinions. To those who have not controlled their own minds this world is either full of evil or a mixture of good and evil. This very world will become an optimistic world when we have become masters of our own minds. Nothing will work upon us as good or evil; we shall find everything harmonious. Some men who begin by saying the world is a hell will end by saying it is heaven. If we are genuine Karma Yogis and want to train ourselves to this state, wherever we may begin we shall end in perfect self-abnegation, and as soon as this seeming self has gone this whole world, which at first appears to us to lie filled with evil, will appear to be heaven and full of blessedness. Its very atmosphere will be blessed; every human face will be good. This is the goal and end of Karma Yoga, and this is perfection. So, you see, these various Yoga's do not conflict with each other; each one goes to the same goal and makes us perfect, but each one has to be practised. The whole secret is in practising. First hear, then think, and then practise. This is true of every Yoga. You have first to hear about it and understand what it is, and many things you do not understand, by constant hearing, will be made clear. It is hard to understand everything at once. The explanation of everything is in yourself. No one was ever taught by another; each one of us has to teach himself. The external teacher is only the suggestion which rouses the internal teacher to understand things. Then things will be made clearer by the power of perception, and we shall realize them in our own souls, and that will become an intense power of will. First feeling, then it becomes willing, and out of that willingness will come the tremendous power of work that will go through every vein, and nerve, and muscle, until the whole mass of your body is changed into that unselfish Yoga of work, and the result will be perfect self-abnegation, utter unselfishness. It does not depend on any dogma, or doctrine, or belief; either Christian, or Jew, or Gentile, it does not matter. Are you unselfish? That is the question. If you are, you will be perfect without reading a single religious book, without going into a single church or temple. "Fools alone say that work and philosophy are different, not the learned." The learned know that, though apparently different from each other, they at last come to the same goal, and that is perfection.

VII. FREEDOM

In addition to meaning work, we have seen that the word Karma also means causation. Any work, any action, any thought, that produces an effect is called a Karma. This law of Karma means the law of causation; wheresoever there is a cause, an effect must be produced; it cannot be resisted, and that law of Karma, according to our philosophy, is pervading the whole universe. Whatever we see, or feel, or do; whatever action there is anywhere in the universe, is but the effect of past work on the one hand, and, on the other hand, becomes the cause, and produces another effect. It is necessary, together with this, to consider the word law. We see psychologically that law is the tendency of a series to repeat itself. When we see one event followed by another, or sometimes happening simultaneously, we expect this will always follow. A series of phenomena become associated in our mind in a sort of invariable order, so that what we see at one time immediately refers to other facts in the mind. One idea, or, according to our psychology, one wave, produced in the mind stuff, always produces many similar ones. This is the law of association, and causation is only a part of this law of pervasive association. In the external world the idea of law is the same as in the internal world the expectation that one phenomenon will be followed by another, and that the series will repeat itself, so far as we can see. Really speaking, therefore, law does not exist in nature. Practically, it is an error to say that gravitation exists in the earth, or that there is any law existing anywhere in nature. Law is the method, the manner in which our mind grasps a series of phenomena; it is all in the mind. Certain phenomena happening together, followed by the conviction with which our mind grasps the whole series, is what we call law.

The next question will be what we mean by law being universal. Our universe is that portion of existence which is cut off by what the Sanskrit psychologists call "Nama-Rupa" (name and form). This universe is only one part of that infinite existence, which has been thrown into a peculiar mould, or that is composed of name and form, and when it fills that mould that part of the sum total of existence which fills the mould is what is called our universe. It necessarily follows that law is only possible within this universe; beyond that there cannot be any law. When we speak of this universe, we only mean that portion of existence which is limited by our mind; the universe of senses, which we can see, feel, touch, hear, think of, imagine; that portion of the universe alone is under law, but beyond that it cannot be under law, because causation does not extend beyond that. Anything beyond the range of our mind and our senses is not bound by the law of causation, as there is no association beyond the senses, and no causation without association of ideas. It is only when it gets moulded into name and form that existence obeys the law of causation, and is said to be under law, because law has its essence in causation. Therefore, we see at once that there cannot be any free will; the very words are a contradiction, because will is what we know, and everything that we know is within our universe, and everything within our universe has been moulded into name and form, and everything that we know, or can possibly know, must obey causation, and that which obeys the law of causation cannot be free. It is acted upon by other agents, and becomes cause in turn, and so on. But that which became converted into the will, which was not the will, but which, when it fell into this mould, became converted into the human will, is free, and when this will get out of this mould of causation it will be free again. From freedom it comes, and becomes moulded into this bondage, and it gets out and goes back to freedom.

The question was raised, "From whom this universe comes, in whom it rests, and to whom it goes?" The answer was given, "From that Freedom it comes, it rests in bondage, and it goes back into that Freedom." So, when we speak of man as that being who is manifesting, only one part is man; this body and this mind which we see are only one part of the whole man, only one spot of that infinite Being which is man. This whole universe is only one speck of the infinite Being, and all our laws, and our bondages, our joys and our sorrows, our happiness's, and our expectations, are only within this small universe, all our progression and digression are within this small space. Thus, you see how childish it is to expect a continuation of this world, to expect and hope to go to heaven, which means a repetition of this world that we have. You see at once that it is an impossible and childish desire to make the whole infinite universe conform to that existence which we know. When a man says he will have this thing again and again which he is having now, or, as I sometimes say, when he asks for a comfortable religion, you may know that he has become so degenerate that he cannot think of anything higher than he is now, just his little present surroundings. He has forgotten his infinite nature, and his whole idea is confined to these little joys and sorrows, and jealousies of the moment. He thinks this is the infinite, and not only so, he will not let it go. He clings on desperately to "Trishna," the thirst after life. There are millions of happiness's, and beings, and laws, and progresses, and causations all acting apart from what we know. This is but one section of our infinite nature.

To acquire freedom, we have to get beyond this universe; it cannot be found here. Perfect equilibrium cannot be attained in this universe, nor in heaven, nor earth, nor anywhere where thoughts can go, or the mind, where the senses can feel, see, hear or touch, or which we can imagine. No such place can give freedom, because it would be all within our universe, and that universe must be bound by causation. It may be much finer than this; there are places that are much finer than this earth of ours, where enjoyments will be keener, but it will be in the universe, and therefore in bondage, so we will have to go beyond, and real religion begins there, where this little universe ends. Where these little joys, and sorrows, and knowledges end, there the Real begins. Until we can give up this thirst after life, this strong attachment to this existence of one moment, we have no hope of catching even a glimpse of that infinite freedom beyond. It stands then that there is only one way to attain to that freedom which is the goal of mankind, and that is by giving up this little life, giving up this little universe, giving up this earth, giving up heaven, giving up the body, giving up the mind, giving up everything. If we can give up this little universe of the senses, or the mind, immediately we shall be free. The only way to come out of bondage is to go beyond law, go beyond causation, and wherever this universe exists, there causation prevails.

But it is the most difficult thing to give up this universe; few ever attain to that. There are two ways in our books. One is called the "Neti Neti" (not this, not this), the negative; and the other is called the "Iti Iti" (this, this), the positive way. The negative way is the most difficult. It is only possible to the very highest, exceptional minds, with gigantic will powers, who simply stand and say, "No, I will not have this," and the mind and body obey, and they come out. But such people are very rare, and the vast majority of mankind choose the positive way, the way through this world, making use of all the bondages themselves to break those bondages. That is also giving up, only slowly and gradually, by knowing things, enjoying things, and thus, getting experience, and knowing the nature of things, until the mind lets them go away and becomes unattached. The one is by reasoning and the other is through work. The first is for the Jnani, and is by refusing to work, and the second is Karma Yoga, by working. Everyone must work in the universe. "Only those who are perfectly satisfied with the Self, whose desires do not go beyond the Self, whose mind never strays out of the Self, to whom that Self is all in all, do not work." The rest must all work. A current rushing down stream of its own nature, falls into a hollow and makes a whirlpool, and, after running a little in that whirlpool, it emerges again in the form of the free current. So, each human life is like that current. It gets into the whirl, gets involved in this world of name and form, whirls round a little, crying, my father, my brother, my name, my fame, and at last emerges, and regains its freedom. The whole universe is doing that, whether it knows it or not. Everyone is having this experience, consciously or unconsciously, and in the long run getting out of this whirlpool.

But what is Karma Yoga? Knowing the secret of work. We see that the whole universe is working. For what? For salvation, for liberty, from the atom to the highest being working for that one end, liberty for the mind, for the body, for the spirit, for everything; always trying to get freedom, flying away from bondage. The sun, moon, earth, the planets, are all trying to fly from bondage. Karma Yoga tells us the secret, the method of work. Instead of being knocked about in this universe, and after long delay and thrashing, getting to know things as they are, Karma Yoga teaches us the secret of work, the method of work, the organizing power of work. The vast mass of energy may be spent in vain, if we do not know how to utilize it. Karma Yoga makes a science of it; you learn how to utilize all the workings of this world. Work is inevitable, it must be, but work to the highest purpose. Karma Yoga makes us admit that this world is a world of five minutes; that it is something we have to pass through; that real freedom is not here, but we must go beyond to come to freedom. To find the way out we will have to go through it slowly and surely. There may be those exceptional persons about whom I just spoke, who can stand aside and give it up, as a snake casts off its skin and stands aside and looks at it; there are some of these exceptional beings; but for the rest of mankind, they have to slowly go through it, and Karma Yoga shows to the world the process, the secret, the method of doing it to the best advantage.

What does it say? "Work thou incessantly but give up all attachment to work." Do not identify yourself with anything. Hold your mind free. All this that you see, the pains and the miseries, are but conditions of this world; poverty and wealth, and happiness, are but momentary; they do not belong to our nature at all. Our nature is far beyond misery, or happiness, beyond everything of the senses, beyond the imagination; and yet we must go on working all the time. "Misery comes through attachment, not through work." As soon as we identify ourselves with the work, we feel miserable, but if we do not identify ourselves with it, we do not feel that misery. If a beautiful picture belonging to another is burned, a man does not become miserable, but when his own picture is burned how miserable he feels! Why? Both were beautiful pictures, perhaps copies of the same original, but in one case misery is felt and not in the other. It is because in one case he identifies himself with the picture, and not in the other. This "I and mine" causes the whole misery. With possession came selfishness, and selfishness brought misery. Every act of selfishness or thought of selfishness makes us attached to something behind, and immediately we are made slaves. Each wave in the *Chitta* that says, "I and mine," immediately puts a chain round us and makes us slaves, and the more we say "I and mine" the more slavery grows, the more misery increases. Therefore, Karma Yoga tells us to enjoy all the pictures in the world, but not to identify ourselves with them. Never say "Mine." Whenever we say a thing is ours, misery will immediately come. Do not even say "My child" in your mind. Enjoy the child, but do not say "Mine." If you do, then will come the misery. Do not say "My house," do not say "My body." The whole difficulty is there. The body is neither yours nor mine nor anybody's. These bodies are coming and going by the laws of nature, but we are free, standing as witness. This body is no more free than a picture, or the wall. Why should we attach ourselves to a body? If somebody paints a picture, he does it and passes away. Why be attached to it? Let it pass. Do not project that tentacle of selfishness, "I will possess it." As soon as that is projected misery will begin.

So, the Karma Yogi says, first destroy the tendency to project this tentacle of selfishness, and when you have the power of checking that, hold it in, do not allow the mind to get into that sort of wave. Then go out into the world and work as much as you can. Mix everywhere; go where you please; you will never be touched. Like the lotus leaf in water, which the water cannot wet, so will you be. This is called "Vairâghyam." It is the law of Karma Yoga, non-attachment. I have just told you that without non-attachment there cannot be any Yoga. It is the basis of all the Yogas, and this is the real meaning of non-attachment; the man who gives up living in houses, and wearing fine clothes, and eating good food, and goes into the desert, may be a most attached person. His only possession, his own body, may become everything to him, and he is struggling for his body. Non-attachment does not mean what we do in our external body, but it is in the mind; this connecting link of "I and mine" is in the body. If we have not this link with the body, and with things of the senses, we are non-attached, wherever we be. A man may be on a throne and perfectly non-attached; another man may be in rags and still very much attached. First, we attain to this non-attachment, and then we work incessantly. Karma

Yoga gives a method to help us in giving up this attachment. It is hard to give it up.

Here are the two ways of giving up all attachment. The one is for those who do not believe in God, or in any outside help. They are left to their own devices; they have simply to work with their own will, the power of the mind, that "I must be non-attached," and with the power of discrimination. For those who believe in God, it is less difficult. They give up the fruits of work unto the Lord, and then go to work and are never attached to the results. Whatever they see, feel, hear, do, is for Him. Whatever good work we do, let us not take any praise to ourselves. It is the Lord's; give up the fruits unto Him. The grandest works that we do in our lives, never let us think that we shall receive the benefits thereof, or that we have done a good work. Let us be at peace, perfect peace, with ourselves, and give up our whole body and mind and everything as an eternal sacrifice. Instead of the sacrifice of pouring oblations into the fire, make this one great sacrifice day and night the sacrifice of the little self. Day and night renounce the seeming self until it becomes a habit, until it gets into the blood, the nerves, the brain, and the whole body is every moment obedient to this idea. Then we can get out anywhere, nothing will touch us. Go into the midst of the battlefield, with roaring cannon and the din of war, and we shall be free and at peace.

Karma Yoga teaches us duty as on the lower plane; each one of us must do his duty. This is my duty, and that is my duty. Yet we see that this duty is the one great cause of misery. It becomes a disease with us, drags us ever forward. It clutches hold of us and makes our whole life miserable. It is the bane of human life. "This idea of duty is the mid-day summer sun which scorches the innermost soul of mankind." Look at those poor slaves to duty. Duty leaves them no time to think of anything else, no time to say prayers, no time to bathe. Duty is ever on them. They go out and work. Duty is on them. They come home and think of the work for next day. Duty is on them! It is living a slave's life, at last dropping down in the street and dying in harness, like a horse. This is duty as it is understood. The only duty is to be unattached and to work as free beings. Blessed are we that we are here. We serve our time; whether we do it ill or well, who knows? If we, do it well, we do not get the reward. If we, do it ill, neither do we get the punishment. Be at rest, be free, and work. This is a very hard thing to attain. How easy it is to interpret slavery as duty the morbid attachment of flesh for flesh as duty! Men go out into the world and struggle and fight for money. Ask them why they do it. They say:" It is a duty." It is the absurd greed for gold, and they want to cover it with a few flowers.

What is duty, after all? It is this impulsation of the flesh, our attachment; and when an attachment has been established, we call it duty. For instance, in countries where there is no marriage, there is no duty between husband and wife; when marriage comes and husband and wife live together, they live together on account of flesh attachment, and that becomes settled after generations, and when it becomes settled it becomes a duty. It is a sort of chronic disease. When it is acute, we call it a disease, when it is chronic, we call it nature. But it is a disease just the same. So, when attachment becomes chronic, we baptize it with the high-sounding name of duty. We strew flowers upon it, trumpets sound, sacred texts are said over it, and then the whole world fights, and each one robs the other for this duty's sake. Duty is good; it checks brutality to a certain extent. To the lowest men, who cannot have any other ideal, it is of some good, but those who want to be Karma Yogis must throw this idea of duty overboard. There is no duty for you and me. Whatever you have to give to the world, give, but not as a duty. Do not take any thought of that. Be not compelled. Why should you be compelled? Everything that you do under compulsion is attachment. Why should you have any duty? You have no duty under the sun. If you want reward, you must also have punishment; the only way to get out of the punishment is to give up the reward. The only way of getting out of misery is by giving up the idea of happiness, because these two are linked to each other. On one side happiness, on the other misery. On one side life, on the other death. The only way to get beyond death is to give up life; not to care for it. Life and death are the same thing, looked at from different points. So, the idea of happiness without misery, or life without death is very good for schoolboys and children, but the thinker sees that it is a contradiction of terms and gives up both. Seek no praise, no reward, for anything you do. It is a very hard task. No sooner do we do a good action than we begin to desire credit for it. No sooner do we give money to some charity than we want to see our names in the papers. Misery must come as the result of such desires. The greatest men in the world have passed away unknown. The Buddhas and the Christs that you see are but second-degree men in comparison with them. Hundreds of them have lived in every country, working silently. Silently they pass away, and in time their thoughts find expression in Buddhas or Christs, and the latter become known to us. The highest men did not seek to get any name or fame from their knowledge. Their whole nature shrank from it. They are the pure Sattvikis, who can never make any stir, but melt down in love.

Next in order come men with more Rajas, or activity, combative natures, who take up the ideas of the perfect ones and preach them to the world. These highest ones silently collect ideas and the others, the Buddhas and Christs, go from place-to-place preaching and working. The highest men are calm, silent and unknown. They are the men who really know the power of thought; they are sure that even if they go into a cave and close up the door, simply think five thoughts and pass away, these five thoughts will live through eternity. They will penetrate through the mountains and cross oceans, and travel through the world, and will enter into some brain and raise up some man who will give expression to these thoughts. These men are too near the Lord to become active and fight, working, struggling, preaching, and doing good to humanity. The active workers, however good, have still a little remnant of ignorance. When our nature has yet some impurities left, then alone can we work. The highest men cannot work. "Those who's whole soul is gone into the Self, those whose desires are confined in the Self, who have become ever associated with the Self, for them there is no work." So, these are the highest of mankind, who cannot work; but aside from these, everyone has to work. But never think that you can help the least thing in this universe. You cannot. You only help yourself in this gymnasium of the world. This is the attitude of work. If you work in this way; if you always remember that it is a privilege which has been given you, you will never be attached. This world goes on. Millions like you and me think we are great people in the world, but we die, and in five minutes the world has forgotten us. Give up all fruits of work; do good for good's sake; then alone will come perfect non-attachment. The bonds of the heart will break, and we shall reap perfect freedom. This is the secret of Karma.

VIII. The Ideal of Karma Yoga

The idea is that we are to reach the same goal by different means, and these means I generalize into four work, love, psychology and knowledge. But you must, at the same time, remember that these divisions are not very marked. Each blend into the other, but as the type prevails the divisions come. It is not that you cannot find a man who has no other faculty excepting that of work, or that you cannot find men who are more than worshippers only, nor men who have more than knowledge. These divisions are made on account of the type or tendency that predominates in a man. We have found that, in the end, they all converge and become one: reaching one goal. All religions and all methods of work are going towards that goal.

First, I will try to point out the goal. What is the goal of the whole universe? Freedom. Everything that we see, feel, hear is struggling towards freedom, from the atom to the man, from the insentient, lifeless particle of matter to the highest human existence, the human soul. The whole universe is the result of this struggle for freedom. In all these combinations every particle is trying to fly from the other particles, and the others are holding it in check. Our earth is trying to fly from the sun and the moon from the earth. Everything has a tendency to infinite dispersion. All that we see in this universe, good, bad or indifferent, all the work or thought that is in this universe, has for its basis this one struggle towards freedom; it is under the impulse of this that the saint prays, and the robber robs. When the line of action taken is not a proper one, we call it evil, and when the manifestation is proper and high, we call it good. But the impulse is the same, to struggle towards that freedom. The saint is oppressed with the idea of his bondage, and he wants to get rid of it, so he worships God. The thief is oppressed with the idea that he does not possess certain things, and he wants to get rid of that, to get freedom from it, so he steals. Freedom is the one goal of all nature, sentient or insentient, and, consciously or unconsciously, everything is struggling towards that.

We find in every religion the manifestation of this struggle towards freedom. It is the groundwork of all morality, of unselfishness, which means getting out of the idea that I am this little body. When we see a man doing good work, helping others, it means that that man will not be confined within the limited circle of "me and mine." There is no limit to this getting out. All the great systems of ethics preach absolute unselfishness as the goal. Supposing this absolute unselfishness can be reached by a man, what becomes of that man? He is no more that little Mr. So-and-So; he has acquired infinite expansion. That little personality which he had before is lost forever; he has become infinite, and the attainment of this infinite expansion is the goal of all religions and of all teachings. The personalist, when he hears the idea philosophically put, gets frightened. At the same time, when he is preaching morality, he is preaching the very same thing. He puts no limit to the unselfishness of man. Suppose a man becomes perfectly unselfish under the personalistic system, how are we to distinguish him from others in other systems? He is one with the universe, and that is the goal, only the poor personalist dares not follow out his own premises to their right conclusion. Karma Yoga is attaining this goal through unselfish work, that freedom which is the goal of human nature. Every selfish action, therefore, retards our reaching the goal, and every unselfish action takes us towards the goal; that is why the only definition that can be given of morality is this that which is selfish is immoral, and that which is unselfish is moral.

But, if you come to the details, you will find a difference. For instance, environment will make the details different. The same action under one set of circumstances will be unselfish, and under another set will be selfish, so we can give only a general definition and leave the details to be worked out by the difference in time, place and circumstance. In one country one sort of behaviour will be considered moral, and in another very immoral, because the circumstances differ. We find that the goal of all nature is freedom, and that this freedom is only to be attained by perfect unselfishness, and every action, thought, word or deed that is unselfish takes us towards the goal and, as such, is called moral. That definition, you will find, will hold good for every religion and every system of ethics. For instance, you will find different ideas of ethics. In some systems they are derived from a superior Being, God. If you ask why a man shall do this and not do that they will answer, because it is the command of God. But whatever be the source from which it is derived, their code of ethics will have as the one central idea not to think of self, to give up self. And yet some of them with this high ethical idea are frightened to give up their little personalities. I would ask the man who would cling to the little personalities to consider the case of a man who has become perfectly unselfish, who has no thought for himself, who does no deed for himself, who speaks no word for himself, where then is "himself?" That "himself" is personal to him so long as he thinks, acts and knows for himself. If he is only conscious of others, of the universe, where is "himself?" It is gone forever.

This Karma Yoga, therefore, is a system to attain to freedom through unselfishness, by good works. The Karma Yogi need not have any doctrine whatever. He may not believe in a God, may not ask what his soul is or think of any metaphysical speculation. He has got his special task; he has got to work it out himself. Every moment of his life must be realization because he is working out, without a doctrine or theory, the very same problem that the Jnani or the worshipper speculates upon and formulates as doctrines.

Now comes the next question. What is this work? What is this doing good to the world? Can we do good to the world? In an absolute sense, no; in a relative sense, yes. No permanent good can be done to this world; if it could be it would not be this world. We can satisfy the hunger of a man for five minutes, and he will be hungry again. Every pleasure with which we can supply a man can only be momentary. No one can permanently cure this ever-recurring series of pleasure and pain. Can any permanent mass of happiness be given to the world? No, not even that. In the ocean you cannot raise one wave without making a hollow somewhere else. The sum total of the energies in the world is the same throughout, always the same. It cannot be increased or decreased. Take the history of the human race as we know it today. The same miseries and the same happiness's, the same pleasure and pain, the same differences in position; some rich, some poor, some high in position, some low, some healthy, some unhealthy. You find it was just the same with the ancient Egyptians, the Greeks, the Romans, as with the Americans to-day. So far as history is known it has always been the same; yet, at the same time, we find that, running along with all these differences of pleasure and pain, there has ever been the struggle to alleviate it. At every period of history there have been thousands of men and women who have been struggling to smooth the passage of life of others. And they have never succeeded. We can only play at driving the ball from one place to another. We take pain from the physical body, and it goes to the mental body. It is like that picture in Dante's hell where the misers were given a mass of gold. They began pushing it up the hill, and again it rolled down. Thus this wheel is going on. All these talks about a millennium are very nice as schoolboys' stories, but no better than that. All nations that dream of millenniums also think that they will have the best of it at that time; this is the wonderfully unselfish idea of this millennium!

We come to this, that we cannot add happiness to this world; similarly, we cannot add pain. The sum total of the energies displayed will be the same throughout. We just push it from this side to the other side, and from that side to this, but it will remain the same, because it is its very nature. This ebb and flow, this rising and falling, is its very nature; it would be as logical to say we can have life without death. It is complete nonsense, because the very idea of life is constant death. The lamp is constantly burning out, and that is its life. If you want life you will have to die every moment also. These are only different expressions of the same thing, looked at from different standpoints; each of them is the falling and the rising of the same wave, and the two form one link. One looks at the "fall" side and becomes a pessimist or at the "rise" side and becomes an optimist. When a boy is going to school and his father and mother are taking care of him everything seems blessed to him; his wants are simple; he is a great optimist. But the old man, with his experience, has become calmer, and he has cooled down. So old nations, with decay all around them, are less hopeful than new nations. There is a proverb in India: "A thousand years a city and a thousand years a forest." This change is going on, and it makes people optimists or pessimists according to the side they see.

The next idea we will take up is the idea of equality. These millennium ideas have been great motive powers to work. Many religions preach this as an element. God is coming to rule the universe; there will be no difference in conditions. The people who preach this are fanatics, and fanatics are the sincerest of mankind. Christianity was preached just on this fanaticism, and that was what made it attractive to the Greek slaves and the Roman slaves. They believed they would have no more slavery, plenty to eat and drink, and therefore they flocked round the standard. Those who preached the idea first were, of course, ignorant fanatics, but very sincere. In modern times it takes the form of equality, liberty and fraternity. This is also fanaticism. This equality has never been and never can be. How could you be equal here? That would be death. What makes this world? Lost balance. In the primal state, which is called Chaos, there is perfect balance. How do all these forces come? By struggling, competition, conflict. Suppose all these particles of matter were held in equilibrium, would there be creation? We know from science there would not be. Disturb the water, and you find every particle of water trying to become calm again, one rushing against the other, and in this way come all these phenomena which you call the universe all things are struggling to get back to the state of perfect balance. Then again, a disturbance will come, and this combination will go on, making creation. Inequality is the very basis of creation. At the same time, the forces struggling to obtain equality are as much a necessity of creation as those which destroy it.

Absolute equality, that which means a perfect balance of all the struggling forces, will never be in this world. Before you have attained to that state the world will have cooled down and become a lump of ice, and no one will be here. We find, therefore, that all these ideas of millennium, or absolute equality, are not only impossible, but, if we could carry them out, they would lead to the day of destruction. There is, again, the difference in the brains of men. What makes the difference between man and man? It is the difference in the brain. Nowadays no one but a lunatic will say we are all born with the same brain power. We have come into the world as unequal; we have come as greater men or as lesser men, and there is no getting away from that. The American Indians were in this country for thousands of years, and a few handfuls of your ancestors came. What made all this difference, if we are all the same? Why could not the Indians have made improvements and built cities, why did they only go about hunting in the forests all the time, if we are all equal? A different sort of brain matter came, different bundles of past impressions came, and they worked out and manifested themselves. Absolute non-differentiation is death. So long as this world lasts, this differentiation will be, but the millennium will come, when the cycle comes to an end. Before that equality cannot be. Yet this idea is a great motive power. Just as this inequality is necessary for creation, so the struggle to limit it is necessary. If there were no differentiation, there would be no creation; if there were no struggle to become free and get back there would be no creation; but it is the difference between the two forces that makes the motive power. There will, therefore, always be these motive powers to work.

This wheel within wheel is terrible mechanism; if we put our hands in, as soon as we are caught, we are gone. Each one of us thinks that when we have done a certain duty, we will be at rest, but before we have done a part of that, another is waiting. We are all being dragged along by this machine. There are only two ways; one is to give up the machine, to let go, and stand aside. Give up our desires. That is very easy to say, but it is almost impossible to do. I do not know whether in twenty million's of men one can do that. The other way is to plunge into the world and learn the secret of work, and that is Karma Yoga. Do not fly from it but stand inside and know the secret of work. Through work we shall come out. Through that machinery is the way out.

We have now seen what this work is. To sum up the whole thing, this work goes on all the time, and those that believe in a God will understand it better by thinking that God is not such an incapable person as to require our help. Secondly, this universe will go on always. We must remember that our goal is freedom; our goal is unselfishness, and that goal is to be reached through work, and, therefore, we must learn the secret of work. So far, we have learnt that this work goes on; all such ideas as of making this world perfectly happy may be good as motive powers, for fanatics; such silly ideas may have been good in old times, but we must always know that, although fanaticism is a very good motive power, and does some good work, at the same time it brings as much evil as good. The Karma Yogi asks why should you require any motive to work? Be beyond motives. "To work you have the right, but not to the fruits thereof." Man can train himself to that, says the Karma Yogi. When the idea of doing good will come into his very being, then he will not seek for any motive outside. Why shall we do good? Because we like and ask no questions. Do good because it is good to do good; he who does good work in order to get to heaven binds himself, says the Karma Yogi. Any work that is done with a motive, instead of making us free, which is the goal, makes one more chain for our feet. If we think by such and such work we shall get to heaven, we shall be attracted to a place called heaven, and we shall have to go and see all these things; that will be one more bondage.

So the only way is to give up all the fruits of work; be non-attached. Know that this world is not we, or we this world; that we are really not the body; that we really do not work. We are the Self, eternally at rest and at peace. Why should we be bound by anything? We must not weep; there is no weeping for the Soul. We must not even weep for sympathy. Only, we like that sort of thing, and, in our imagination, we think that God is weeping in that way on His throne. Such a God would not be worth attaining. Why should God weep at all? It is a sign of weakness, of bondage. There should not be a drop of tears. How can it be done? It is very good to say be perfectly non-attached, but what is the way to do it? Every good work we do without any ulterior motive, instead of forging a chain, will break one of the links in our chain. Every good thought that we send to the world, without thinking of the return, will be stored up, and break one link in the chain, and make us purer, until we become the purest of mortals. Yet it seems to be rather quixotic and philosophical, than practical. I have read many arguments against the Gita, and many have raised the argument that without motive you cannot work. They have never seen work, except fanaticism, and, therefore, speak in that way.

I will tell you in a few words about one man who carried non-attachment into practice. That man was Buddha. He is the one man who ever carried this into perfect practice. All the prophets of the world, except Buddha, had external motive power to move them. The prophets of the world, with his exception, can be divided into two sets, one set who say they are God come down on earth, and the other who say they are messengers from God; and both draw their impetus from outside, expect reward from outside, however spiritual may be the language they use. But Buddha is the only prophet who said "I do not care to know your various theories about God. What is the use of discussing all the subtle doctrines about the soul? Do good and be good. And this will take you to whatever truth there is." He was absolutely without external motive power, and what man worked more than he? Show me in history one character who went so high above all. The whole human race has produced but one such character; such high philosophy; such sympathy; this great philosopher, preaching the highest philosophy, and yet having sympathy for the lowest animals, and never making any claims. He is the ideal Karma Yogi, acting entirely without personal motive, and the history of humanity shows him to have been the greatest man ever born; beyond compare of all others, the greatest combination of heart and brain that ever existed, the greatest soul-power that was ever manifested. He was the first great reformer the world ever saw. He was the first who dared to say, "Believe not because some old manuscripts are produced, believe not because it is your national belief, because you have been made to believe from your childhood, but reason truth out, and after you have analysed it, then, if you find it will do good to one and all, believe it, live up to it, and help others to live up to it." He works best who works without any selfish motive, desiring neither money nor anything else, and when a man can do that, he, too, will be a Buddha, and out of him will come the power to work in such a manner as to transform the world. This is the very ideal of Karma Yoga.

LIST OF TITLES WITH ISBN NO.

ISBN	TITLE
9788194914129	1984
9789390575220	1984 & Animal Farm (2In1)
9789390575572	1984 & Animal Farm (2In1): The International Best-Selling Classics
9789390575848	35 Sonnets
9789390575329	A Clergyman's Daughter
9789390575923	A Study In Scarlet
9789390896097	A Tale Of Two Cities
9789390896837	Abide in Christ
9789390896202	Abraham Lincoln
9789390896912	Absolute Surrender
9789390896608	African American Classic Collection
9789390575305	Aldous Huxley: The Collected Works
9789390896141	An Autobiography of M. K. Gandhi
9789390575886	Animal Farm
9789390575619	Animal Farm & The Great Gatsby (2In1)
9789390575626	Animal Farm & We
9789390896158	Anna Karenina
9789390575534	Antic Hay
9789390896165	Antony & Cleopatra
9789390896172	As I Lay Dying
9789390896226	As You like it
9789390575671	At Your Command
9789390575350	Awakened Imagination
9789390575114	Be What You Wish
9789390896233	Believe In yourself
9789390896998	Best of Charles Darwin: The Origin of Species & Autobiography
9789390896684	Best Of Horror : Dracula And Frankenstein
9789390575503	Best Of Mark Twain (The Adventures of Tom Sawyer AND The Adventures of Huckleberry Finn)
9789390896769	Black History Collection
9789390575756	Brave New World, Animal Farm & 1984 (3in1)

9789390896240	Brother Karamzov
9789390575053	Bulleh Shah Poetry
9789390575725	Burmese Days
9789390896257	Bushido
9789390896066	Can't Hurt Me
9788194914112	Chanakya Neeti: With The Complete Sutras
9789390896042	Crime and Punishment
9789390575527	Crome Yellow
9789390575046	Down and Out in Paris and London
9789390896844	Dracula
9789390575442	Emersons Essays: The Complete First & Second Series (Self-Reliance & Other Essays)
9789390575749	Emma
9789390575817	Essential Tozer Collection - The Pursuit of God & The Purpose of Man
9789390896578	Fascism What It Is and How to Fight It
9789390575688	Feeling is the Secret
9789390575190	Five Lessons
9789390575954	Frankenstein
9789390575237	Franz Kafka: Collected Works
9789390575282	Franz Kafka: Short Stories
9789390575060	George Orwell Collected Works
9789390575077	George Orwell Essays
9789390575213	George Orwell Poems
9788194914150	Greatest Poetry Ever Written Vol 1
9788194914143	Greatest Poetry Ever Written Vol 1
9789390896301	Gulliver's Travel
9789390575961	Gunaho Ka Devta
9789390575893	H. P. Lovecraft Selected Stories Vol 1
9789390575978	H. P. Lovecraft Selected Stories Vol 2
9789390896059	Hamlet
9789390575022	His Last Bow: Some Reminiscences of Sherlock Holmes
9789390896134	History of Western Philosophy
9789390575121	Homage To Catalonia

9789390896219	How to develop self-confidence and Improve public Speaking
9789390896295	How to enjoy your life and your Job
9789390575633	How to own your own mind
9789390896318	How to read Human Nature
9789390896325	How to sell your way through the life
9789390896370	How to use the laws of mind
9789390896387	How to use the power of prayer
9789390896028	How to win friends & Influence People
9788194824176	How To Win Friends and Influence People
9789390896103	Humility The Beauty of Holiness
9789390896653	Imperialism the Highest Stage of Capitalism
9789390575084	In Our Time
9789390575169	In Our Time & Three Stories and Ten poems
9789390575145	James Allen: The Collected Works
9789390896189	Jesus Himself
9789390575480	Jo's Boys
9789390896394	Julius Caesar
9789390575404	Keep the Aspidistra Flying
9789390896400	Kidnapped
9789390896424	King Lear
9789390575824	Lady Susan
9789390896455	Law of Success
9789390896264	Lincoln The Unknown
9789390575565	Little Men
9789390575640	Little Women
9788194914174	Lost Horizon
9789390896462	Macbeth
9789390896929	Man Eaters of Kumaon
9789390896523	Man The Dwelling Place of God
9789390896349	Man The Dwelling Place of God
9789390575909	Mansfield Park
9788194914136	Manto Ki 25 Sarvshreshth Kahaniya
9789390896509	Marxism, Anarchism, Communism
9789390575664	Mathematical Principles of Natural Philosophy

9788194914198	Meditations
9789390575800	Mein Kampf
9789390575794	Memory How To Develop, Train, And Use It
9789390896486	Mind Power
9789390896585	Money
9789390575039	Mortal Coils
9789390575770	My Life and Work
9789390896035	Narrative of the Life of Frederick Douglass
9789390575152	Neville Goddard: The Collected Works
9789390575985	Northanger Abbey
9789390896530	Notes From Underground
9789390896547	Oliver Twist
9789390575459	On War
9789390575541	One, None and a Hundred Thousand
9789390896554	Othelo
9789390575435	Out Of This World
9789390575015	Persuasion
9789390575510	Prayer The Art Of Believing
9789390575091	Pride and Prejudice
9789390896561	Psychic Perception
9789390575381	Rabindranath Tagore - 5 Best Short Stories Vol 2
9789390575367	Rabindranath Tagore - Short Stories (Masters Collections Including The Childs Return)
9789390575374	Rabindranath Tagore 5 Best Short Stories Vol 1 (Including The Childs Return
9789390896622	Romeo & Juliet
9789390896127	Sanatana Dharma
9789390575596	Seedtime & Harvest
9789390896639	Selected Stories of Guy De Maupassant
9789390575206	Self-Reliance & Other Essays
9789390575176	Sense and Sensibility
9789390575299	Shyamchi Aai
9789390896738	Socialism Utopian and Scientific
9789390896646	Success Through a Positive Mental Attitude
9789390575428	The Adventures of Huckleberry Finn

9789390575183	The Adventures of Sherlock Holmes
9789390575343	The Adventures of Tom Sawyer
9789390896691	The Alchemy Of Happiness
9789390575862	The Art Of Public Speaking
9789390896288	The Autobiography Of Charles Darwin
9788194914181	The Best of Franz Kafka: The Metamorphosis & The Trial
9789390575008	The Call Of Cthulhu and Other Weird Tales
9789390575107	The Case-Book of Sherlock Holmes
9789390896110	The Castle Of Otranto
9789390896745	The Communist Manifesto
9789390575589	The Complete Fiction of H. P. Lovecraft
9789390575497	The Complete Works of Florence Scovel Shinn
9789390896820	The Conquest of Breard
9789390896813	The Diary of a Young Girl
9789390896332	The Diary of a Young Girl The Definitive Edition of the Worlds Most Famous Diary
9789390575701	The Great Gatsby, Animal Farm & 1984 (3In1)
9789390575312	The Greatest Works Of George Orwell (5 Books) Including 1984 & Non-Fiction
9789390575992	The Hound of Baskervilles
9789390896707	The Idiot
9789390896714	The Invisible Man
9789390575657	The Knowledge of the holy
9789390575558	The Law & the Promise
9789390896721	The Law Of Attraction
9789390896776	The Leader in you
9789390896363	The Life of Christ
9789390896196	The Man-Eating Leopard of Rudraprayag
9789390896783	The Master Key to Riches
9789390575268	The Memoirs Of Sherlock Holmes
9789390896479	The Midsummer Night's Dream
9789390575466	The Mill On The Floss
9789390896790	The Miracles of your mind
9789390896660	The Mutual Aid A Factor in Evolution
9789390896448	The Origin of Species

9789390896905	The Peter Kropotkin Anthology The Conquest of Bread & Mutual Aid A Factor of Evolution
9789390896806	The Picture of Dorian Gray
9789390896271	The Picture of Dorian Gray
9789390575275	The Power Of Awareness
9789390896356	The Power of Concentration
9788194824169	The Power of Positive Thinking
9789390575411	The Power of the Spoken Word
9788194914105	The Power Of Your Subconscious Mind
9789390896899	The Power of Your Subconscious Mind
9789390896417	The Principles of Communism
9789390575787	The Psychology Of Mans Possible Evolution
9789390896615	The Psychology of Salesmanship
9789390575732	The Pursuit of God
9789390575398	The Pursuit of Happiness
9789390896851	The Quick and Easy Way to effective Speaking
9789390575947	The Return Of Sherlock Holmes
9789390575138	The Road To Wigan Pier
9789390896981	The Root of the Righteous
9789390575855	The Science Of Being Well
9788194914167	The Science Of Getting Rich, The Science Of Being Great & The Science Of Being Well (3In1)
9789390896011	The Screwtape Letters
9789390896073	The Screwtape Letters
9789390575336	The Secret Door to Success
9789390575695	The Secret Of Imagining
9789390896868	The Secret Of Success
9789390896431	The Seven Last Words
9789390575930	The Sign of the Four
9789390896004	The Sonnets
9789390896516	The Souls of Black Folk
9789390896875	The Sound and The Fury
9789390575244	The State and Revolution
9789390896882	The Story of My Life
9789390896936	The Story Of Oriental Philosophy

9789390896752	The Strange Case of Dr. Jekyll and Mr. Hyde
9789390896943	The Tempest
9789390575916	The Valley Of Fear
9789390575879	The Wind in the willows
9789390896080	The Wind in the willows
9789390575763	Their eyes were watching gofd
9789390575831	Three Stories
9789390896950	Twelfth Night
9789390896592	Twelve Years a Slave
9789390896677	Up from Slavery
9789390896974	Value Price and Profit
9789390896967	Wake Up and Live
9789390896493	With Christ in the School of Prayer
9789390575602	Your Faith is Your Fortune
9789390575473	Your Infinite Power To Be Rich
9789390575251	Your Word is Your Wand
9789390575718	Youth
9789391316099	A Christmas Carol
9789391316105	A Doll's House
9789391316501	A Passage to India
9789391316709	A Portrait of the Artist as a Young Man
9789391316112	A Tale of Two Cities
9789391316747	A Tear and a Smile
9789391316167	Agnes Gray
9789391316174	Alice's Adventures in Wonderland
9789391316136	Anandamath
9789391316181	Anne Of Green Gables
9789391316754	Anthem
9789391316198	Around The World in 80 Days
9789391316013	As A Man Thinketh
9789391316242	Autobiography of a Yogi
9789391316266	Beyond Good and Evil
9789391316761	Bleak House
9789391316778	Chitra, a Play in One Act
9789391316310	David Copperfield

9789391316075	Demian
9789391316785	Dubliners
9789391316051	Favourite Tales from the Arabian Nights
9789391316235	Gitanjali
9789391316068	Gravity
9789391316150	Great Speeches of Abraham Lincoln
9789391316662	Guerilla Warfare
9789391316839	Kim
9789391316822	Mother
9789391316211	My Childhood
9789391316846	Nationalism
9789391316327	Oliver Twist
9789391316853	Pygmalion
9789391316334	Relativity: The Special and the General Theory
9789391316389	Scientific Healing Affirmation
9789391316341	Sons and Lovers
9789391316587	Tales from India
9789391316372	Tess of The D'Urbervilles
9789391316396	The Awakening and Selected Stories
9789391316402	The Bhagvad Gita
9789391316303	The Book of Enoch
9789391316228	The Canterville Ghost
9789391316907	The Dynamic Laws of Prosperity
9789391316006	The Great Gatsby
9789391316860	The Hungry Stones and Other Stories
9789391316433	The Idiot
9789391316440	The Importance of Being Earnest
9789391316297	The Light of Asia
9789391316914	The Madman His Parables and Poems
9789391316457	The Odyssey
9789391316921	The Picture of Dorian Gray
9789391316464	The Prince
9789391316938	The Prophet
9789391316945	The Republic
9789391316518	The Scarlet Letter

9789391316143	The Seven Laws of Teaching
9789391316525	The Story of My Experiments with Truth
9789391316532	The Tales of the Mother Goose
9789391316549	The Thirty Nine Steps
9789391316594	The Time Machine
9789391316600	The Turn of the Screw
9789391316983	The Upanishads
9789391316617	The Yellow Wallpaper
9789391316426	The Yoga Sutras of Patanjali
9789391316990	Ulysses
9789391316624	Utopia
9789391316679	Vanity Fair
9789391316020	What Is To Be Done
9789391316686	Within A Budding Grove
9789391316693	Women in Love